Pope Benedict XVI

HEINZ-JOACHIM FISCHER

Pope
Benedict XVI

A Personal Portrait

Translated by Brian McNeil

A Crossroad Book
Crossroad Publishing Company
New York

The Crossroad Publishing Company
481 Eighth Avenue, Suite 1550, New York, NY 10001

Originally published as *Benedikt XVI.—Das Porträt*
Herder Verlag, Freiburg, Basle, and Vienna, 2005.

This book is set in 10/15 Adobe Caslon Pro.
The display type is AGaramond.

Printed in the United States of America

Library of Congress Cataloging-in-Publication Data is available

ISBN 0-8245-2372-5

1   2   3   4   5   6   7   8   9   10   09   08   07   06   05

Contents

Contents

Contents

Foreword

THIS WAS ORIGINALLY SUPPOSED to be a book about Joseph Ratzinger, first professor of theology, then cardinal archbishop of Munich, then prefect of the Congregation for the Doctrine of the Faith, and finally dean of the sacred college of cardinals. The book is now completed, and it does speak about this Joseph Ratzinger. But it was recast in the light of his election to the papacy at the age of seventy-eight on April 19, 2005. So momentous was this election that rumors at once started circulating in Rome, spreading the legend that he had already received the necessary majority of two-thirds plus one (77 out of 115 votes) on the third round of voting but that the cardinals chose to wait before making the news known. While there are reasons to doubt this account, it makes a telling point. The eternal city has already welcomed its new bishop with open arms; for as he himself said, he has become "Italianized."

I begin this account with my first meeting with professor Joseph Ratzinger in May 1976 in Regensburg. It was at that time, just as I was beginning my career as a Vatican correspondent, that his stellar career as a theologian and church leader took off. Others will write exhaustively about the youth and early career of the new pope, a chapter that he has also covered in several interviews. While I do have my own experiences of dictatorships, having grown up in communist East Germany, I, nevertheless, decided to write about what I know best about

Joseph Ratzinger—his path from local theologian to world pope and one of the most intriguing thinkers and believers of our day.

I am grateful to the many persons who encouraged me to write and publish this book, for the English language edition in particular to Dr. Gwendolin Herder in New York of The Crossroad Publishing Company, and to the translator, Fr. Brian McNeil. Above all, however, I am grateful to Joseph Ratzinger, now our Holy Father Pope Benedict XVI, for his openness, for all that he has taught me, for the confidence he has shown in me, and for his friendship over almost thirty years. As I recall the many delightful and informal hours we have spent together—sometimes serious, sometimes serene and joyful—I can only express my heartfelt wish that his pontificate may bring blessings to his church and be of benefit to the whole world.

Heinz-Joachim Fischer
May 2005, Rome

Returning to Bavaria

Our First Meeting

I phoned Joseph Ratzinger on April 20, 1976. His telephone number, in Regensburg, Bavaria, Germany, was 0941-91421.

I was on the editorial staff of the *Frankfurter Allgemeine Zeitung* in Frankfurt, and I'd been assigned the job of reporting on the Catholic Church. I was happy to be given this assignment. After studying philosophy and theology at the Pontifical Gregorian University in Rome, I felt reasonably familiar with the subject and well prepared. But I soon realized that while I did not actually become universally disliked, I couldn't please everyone. People who had little contact with church, religion, or Christianity and just wanted basic information quickly suspected me of being too pious—for it was not possible to reduce everything that happened in the church to a question of ecclesiastical or societal politics. And those who were deeply concerned about Christian, religious, and church matters thought I wasn't pious enough, or else not "critical" enough. Among Catholics and other Christians at that time, the latter reproach was heard more and more often.

It was not my job to look for applause, but to report, and as much as possible to avoid offending anyone's sensibilities. For the readers *were* sensitive about religious issues. I began to look for interesting personalities among those professors of theology

1

whom I knew to some extent, and who had earned my respect. One criterion here was the search for candidates for vacant (or soon to be vacated) episcopal sees, candidates for higher things in the church. I spoke with Hans Küng, the rebellious Swiss theologian; with Hans Urs von Balthasar, a man of lyric piety and at the same time a man of immense culture and erudition; and with Karl Lehmann, whom I knew from the year we had spent together as members of the German seminary in Rome.

This was also why I wanted to meet Joseph Ratzinger. He had a rather distinctive reputation as an outsider who nonetheless understood the task of theology as being part of the very heart of Christian faith. Naturally, I didn't mention on the telephone the question of whether he might become a bishop one day. We agreed to meet on May 4, 1976 at four in the afternoon, in the Universitätsstraße 31 in Regensburg. "Drive into the underground parking garage and then make your way to the 'theology' building," he told me.

So that's what I did, on Tuesday May 4, a cool spring day. And I was terribly disappointed. I had imagined Professor Ratzinger's study to be located in some pretty little Baroque or Rococo townhouse. Instead, I had first to navigate my way through a gray labyrinth of terrifying, naked cement corridors and cold cement walls in a modern building that was relatively deserted that afternoon. It took me a long time to find Ratzinger's room. The priest I encountered there was not unfriendly, but he gave me the impression that he could be putting his time to better use than talking to a journalist about theology and the Catholic Church.

There was, however, no immediately "relevant" reason for this interview, nothing controversial that a shy churchman would want to avoid talking about.

We started talking, and the mature professor revealed his fundamental ideas to the journalistic "teenager," who couldn't quite conceal the fact that he had studied in Rome. His deep-set eyes looked at me calmly, then gazed in concentration at some other spot in the room; they never flickered. If I remember correctly, his hair was rather white even then—almost a characteristic mark of the man. He spoke calmly, without getting agitated when he mentioned positions opposed to his own—whether these were held by Catholic or by Protestant theologians, or by sociologists. He seemed sure of the positions he held, and one could follow the compelling logic of his thoughts. If one was disposed to do so, that is. For Joseph Ratzinger was no longer a newcomer to theology.

"Theological teenager"—that's what people had called him in the period of the Second Vatican Council (1962–1965), when Joseph Ratzinger was the theological adviser to Cardinal Frings, Archbishop of Cologne. He was thirty-five years old then, and his ideas made a vital contribution to the renewal of a worldwide church, showed how tensions in Catholic theology could be resolved, and sought cautiously to lay the groundwork for an encounter between the old church and the modern world. The church of the Council owed a great deal of positive inspiration to Ratzinger, to that other "teenager," Hans Küng, and to Karl Rahner, the mentor of German theology. These three consolidated the international fame of German theology and even gave the German bishops the reputation of belonging to the avant-garde.

The Making of a Conservative

In the 1970s, things changed. Ratzinger came to be called a "court theologian" and even to be criticized as a reactionary. His membership in the doctrinal commission of the German bishops indicated that he was one of the most important theologians in the Federal Republic, and his work in the Pontifical International Theological Commission in Rome proved that there was no reason to doubt his orthodoxy. On the other hand, Küng and Rahner, who had once fought on the same side as Ratzinger, kept their distance from both these bodies.

Had the church's theology changed? Or was it Ratzinger who had changed?

In the course of our long conversation, the Catholic dogmatic theologian explained why he had become conservative. This is, in summary, what he told me. Fifteen years ago, at the time of the Council, the battle lines were clearly drawn. On the one side was the Roman school-theology; on the other side, the courageous theologians who dared to engage the world in dialogue. In the last ten years, however, tremendous changes had taken place in the church's dialogue partner, that is, the world. Thanks to the Council's work of opening things up, a vacuum had arisen among educated Catholics: the spiritual elites, for example in the religious orders, had suffered a steep decline in numbers. This made the identity of Christianity fuzzy, and now this identity had to be presented in its clear and distinct outlines. Some had also thought that the simplicity of faith would be enough to cope with the challenge presented by the modern sciences. But the academic work of theology is not so easily and obviously compatible with the spirit of the gospel. Where, he asked, are the great church fathers, who could re-establish a synthesis of faith and reason?

In order to work on this synthesis as an academic theologian, he had withdrawn to his native Bavaria, to the University of Regensburg. Ratzinger said this without bitterness or disappointment, as if he wanted in every situation to make the best of a constellation he disliked. There, in a deeply Catholic land that still retained something of its contemplative character and whose people pride themselves on a down-to-earth common sense—"We let the steeple of our church continue to rise from the center of our village" is one of their proverbs—the Catholic faith might perhaps be more vigorous than in other places. But naturally, even in Bavaria religion had not survived untouched.

From the professor's cold, sterile room, one looked across green meadows to the stately cathedral of Regensburg. Ratzinger mentioned that he felt at ease in the old imperial city, where he had taught theology since 1969. He felt that what he was doing had credibility. He looked back with pleasure to his other universities—to Bonn (1959–1963), Münster (1963–1966), and Tübingen (1966–1969). He enjoyed teaching, but his health was not up to academic politics. Unfortunately, he had very little time for theological research; he traveled a great deal, lecturing in other countries too.

It was possible, of course, that Ratzinger might not remain a professor forever. I was not the only one to see him as destined for the episcopal ministry.

The Episcopal Call

My trip to the Bavarian countryside and my conversation with the enigmatic professor of theology soon proved worthwhile.

At the end of July 1976, Cardinal Julius Döpfner, archbishop of Munich and Freising, died unexpectedly, just sixty-three years old. It proved difficult to find a successor. Then on

March 24, 1977, Pope Paul VI made his decision: Joseph Ratzinger, professor of theology in Regensburg and a man born in Upper Bavaria, was to be entrusted with the most important position in the Catholic Church in southern Germany, by the explicit will of the pope. This immediately shed a favorable light on both the man himself and his views on questions of theology, society, and politics. Ratzinger, not yet fifty years old, became one of the youngest German bishops. His post in Munich meant that he could soon be the dominant figure in German Catholicism as a whole, alongside the cardinal archbishops of Cologne and Berlin.

The moment the prelates in Germany and the Vatican had begun to look for a "worthy and suitable" candidate for the Munich crozier, Ratzinger was regarded as a likely contender. He had been a leading figure in theological discussions in the German-language sphere for many years. The fact that he moved immediately from priest to archbishop, and was created cardinal only a few weeks later, was seen as a promotion issuing from the highest quarters—from the pope himself. It was also interpreted in terms of the Vatican's church politics—it looked like a "Roman" intervention in the German situation.

The new cardinal archbishop had a difficult archdiocese. Administrative tasks, meetings, and time-consuming obligations of various kinds left him no time for tranquil theological research. Joseph Ratzinger had to prove his worth, and opinions in Munich were soon divided. The pope's choice undeniably made some people happy: many Catholics in Munich were content that they had finally gotten a bishop from their own area, after Döpfner, who had come from Franconia.

Others found the appointment hard to accept. Paul VI knew Joseph Ratzinger personally and valued his theological work. Theologians too could recognize in Ratzinger a man with an incomparable knowledge of the intellectual shifts and transformations in the church in recent years, and moreover a man who understood the whole range of problems that these changes entailed. Even his critics had to admit he had had a remarkable career as professor of theology. He lectured on the main subject, Catholic dogmatic theology, in Freising (near Munich) at the tender age of thirty-one, after writing his doctorate under the highly respected professor Gottlieb Söhngen. Only one year later, he was appointed professor at the University of Bonn. During the time of preparation before the Second Vatican Council, the Bavarian theologian delivered a lecture before an audience that included Cardinal Frings of Cologne, who was so impressed by the intellectual brilliance of the young professor that he soon had him appointed a *peritus*, an official papal adviser to the Council.

Ratzinger, however, moved on from his early ideas about what the Council should do. He had insisted that the church must encounter the world and that theology must enter into open debate with the modern sciences. But now he retreated, in what he hoped was an orderly manner that also made sense to others. Doubtless, he felt that the church had taken on more than it could chew, and that the theologians had gotten their fingers burned. As he distanced himself from his audacious ideas, he also distanced himself geographically, after due consideration, from his native province. This is why he had accepted a professorship at the University of Regensburg after his periods at Bonn, Münster, and Tübingen. In Regensburg, the Catholic faith looked more alive than it did elsewhere.

Professor Ratzinger was aware that there was a fine line separating the reactionary who had given up the struggle and the insightful therapist of the contemporary church crisis. As a professor of theology and member of the doctrinal commission of the German bishops and of the papal Theological Commission, he had been the inviolable bulwark of Catholic orthodoxy against attacks from all sides; now, as archbishop, Ratzinger had to be concerned for those Catholics who did not belong to his faithful flock of adherents. His undeniably high intelligence and his winning charm would surely make this task easier for him.

Facing Pastoral Challenges

After he moved into the archbishop's residence, surrounded by big banks on the noble Kardinal-Faulhaber-Straße in Munich, Ratzinger did not always exhibit great ease of manner and deftness of touch in his personal dealings, and this created considerable difficulties for him. As a man from Upper Bavaria and a theological writer who could formulated things in a way the reader understood, he was greatly esteemed by the parish priests in Munich. Unlike his predecessor, Julius Döpfner, however, this new cardinal was definitely not one of the boys, a man who knew how to find the right, easy tone when a group of men came together. It was not surprising that he quickly mastered the business of administration. At the universities, he had always executed such tasks as quickly as possible, with intelligence but without anything resembling enthusiasm for the work of organization. Ratzinger also knew from the outset that he would have a great deal to do in the pastoral sphere in Munich, and this was the main emphasis of his activity in the first period there.

He did not meet with unmixed success. Many things had been neglected in this city of over a million people. Some prelates needed to be prodded into action, but not all took kindly to this; some priests in the archdiocese needed a firm hand, but did not welcome it. Ratzinger knew that exaggerated demands for strict discipline would be counterproductive.

The archbishop was already familiar with the traditional religious customs in Bavaria. It seemed likely that he would give the archdiocese of Munich solid leadership. If the bloom of German Catholicism had somewhat faded, there was a good chance that the cardinal archbishop would help redefine it more clearly and help it become more open. Joseph Ratzinger had to make a synthesis of the high-flying plans of his period as a "theological teenager" with the demanding insights of the post-conciliar years, and that was easier said than done. Not all Catholics were well disposed toward him. In public life, he was respected as an intellectually challenging theologian; a friendly "fisher of men" was needed, but in this area he won few plaudits.

Perhaps mixed results are all that could be achieved in the pastoral work of spreading the faith in the church in those years between 1977 and 1981.

The Call to Rome

The Pope's Candid Theologian

At the end of November, 1981, Pope John Paul II called Cardinal Ratzinger to Rome: the archbishop of Munich was to become prefect of the Vatican Congregation for the Doctrine of the Faith (CDF) and thus head of a papal department that was a bone of contention to many inside and outside the Catholic Church. Historically, this body—as the "Inquisition" or "Holy Office"—had published many verdicts that later generations and even contemporaries found questionable. Not so long ago such critics had included Ratzinger, a *peritus* at the Council, and Cardinal Frings. In theoretical, intellectual terms, the whole thing seemed an anachronism to those who doubted in principle whether it was possible to formulate universally binding principles on questions of faith, morals, and conscience, to analyze these principles, and perhaps even impose them on those who disagreed. In other words, the pope was entrusting the cardinal and theologian Ratzinger with a minefield—both within the church itself and vis-à-vis outsiders.

I myself went on ahead of Ratzinger to Rome, so to speak: I had been writing newspaper reports as a Roman correspondent since 1978, the "year of the three popes," in which I had seen two popes die and two popes elected. I had also seen some-

11

thing of the activity of the Congregation for the Doctrine of the Faith under the Croatian Cardinal Seper, a former student of the German seminary in Rome, with which I had some connections. On the orders of John Paul II, this Vatican body had withdrawn Swiss theologian Hans Küng's authorization as a professor of theology to teach Catholic seminarians in the name of the church. The German bishops had clearly done all they could to reach an amenable solution, but the pope finally lost his patience and empowered the Congregation to "proceed against him"—despite Küng's prestige in public life. Dutch theologian Edward Schillebeeckx was another who felt the power of the Congregation, although he emerged from the process relatively unscathed.

As early as December 1984, after scarcely three years at the head of this Congregation, Cardinal Ratzinger, the German prefect, had obviously lost many friends. The governments of the communist states accused him of profoundly offending them: in an "Instruction" issued by the Congregation for the Doctrine of the Faith in September 1984, he had called communism a "shame of our times" and a "perfidious illusion" that "entire nations are kept in servitude under conditions unworthy of the human person, while it is claimed that they are being brought freedom." Since then, diplomats and representatives of the communist countries had repeatedly made demonstrative complaints in the Vatican, since they took these words as a personal affront. John Paul II, the pope from Poland—still ruled by the communists—also heard complaints from cardinals and archbishops in the Vatican itself. These felt that Ratzinger had at the very least employed a "most undiplomatic" language. The pope smiled quietly to himself and left his chief theologian alone. The pope found the phrase "a shame of our times" an excellent description of communism.

The Fight over Liberation Theology

With the same Instruction, however, the curial cardinal also provoked the ire of those in the West who looked with confidence to the "theology of liberation" to bring salvation to the countries in Latin America (most of which were completely unknown to them). Ratzinger's offense was to condemn "certain forms of the theology of liberation," which he rejected because of the "inspiration they drew from various tendencies of Marxist thought."

In the various conversations I had with him, Cardinal Ratzinger never denied the validity of the fascinating idea that is the starting point of liberation theology, for indeed no Christian could refuse to accept this: namely, that there is an inseparable link between freedom and the Christian religion, closer and more solid than in any other religion (to say nothing of the various ideologies). In Eastertide, Christians recall in a particular way this freedom and liberation, first in the exodus of the people of Israel from Egypt, and ultimately in recalling the death and resurrection of Jesus Christ, which brought freedom from sin and guilt for every human person.

This makes freedom the central idea in Christianity; even in the idea's most profane forms, one cannot deny that the idea of freedom is generated by the spirit of Christianity. In liberation theology, therefore, there was an urgent cry to bring about liberation from poverty and political coercion, from oppression, hunger, and ignorance, and from discrimination of every kind, and all this is a fundamental demand of the Christian faith. Liberation theology demands that honest Christians give their support to every kind of theology that aims to achieve these goals—the theology of liberation and of development, the theology of progress and of revolution.

Did Cardinal Ratzinger strip this basic Christian idea of its power? Did he interrupt the upward flight of the idea of freedom in the spring of that year when he appeared before journalists in Rome like a bookkeeper to analyze liberation theology, finding some elements "completely legitimate, indeed necessary; others a cause for concern; and finally, others unacceptable"? Was he cheating whole peoples in Catholic Latin America of their tremendous hopes? Did this make him disloyal to the new beginnings of the Catholic Church at the Second Vatican Council? These were the penetrating questions we now discussed.

As chief guardian of the doctrinal purity of the Catholic Church, Ratzinger had taken part in a meeting of the Latin American "doctrinal commission," whose members belonged to the various national Catholic episcopal conferences of that continent. As Ratzinger told me in Rome, various "problematic" topics were discussed there: the relationship between bishops and members of religious orders in Latin America; the collaboration between bishops and theologians; the "church of the people" and the "theology of liberation"; questions of moral theology; ecumenism in Latin America, especially in view of the activities of the sects; and general difficulties in pastoral work. It was clear in those contexts that liberation theology was not just a theoretical problem, as it sometimes appeared in Western academic discussions.

We may add that the Catholic Church was never merely a

theological onlooker to the situation in Latin America, as I myself discovered during my travels and research there. Many conversations with bishops, priests, and religious confirmed this point. From the sixteenth century, when missionaries followed on the heels of the conquistadors, up to that day, when pious benedictions were pronounced over bloodthirsty dictators, the church too has been a political actor, and it needed to take responsibility for this history. It would certainly have been possible for supporters of liberation theology, who were then being attacked because of various exaggerations and errors, to reply to their opponents that they themselves shared in the responsibility for the present-day state of affairs, thanks to their "theology of the status quo" or indeed their "theology of oppression," which belonged to the not-too-distant past. But, as Ratzinger said on his return to Rome, blanket accusations do not help anyone—least of all the victims of the situation in Latin America, who all in all have more reason to thank the church than to incriminate it.

Just as the relationship between the Europeans (and North Americans) to the peoples of their former colonies had changed, so the bishops at the Second Vatican Council evoked the rights of those who had so long been oppressed: "It must be a primary concern of the peoples in the developing countries to declare explicitly and decisively that the goal of progress is the full human development of their citizens." Nor was it by chance that many areas of the Third World successfully fought to achieve their independence at precisely that period. In his encyclical *Populorum Progressio* (1967), Pope Paul VI went even further: "People today are yearning for freedom from misery, security of income, health, stable employment conditions, a larger participation in decisionmaking, protection from situations which inflict harm on human dignity, and better education: in a word, to do more, to know more, to have more, and to be more." There can be no doubt that a pope and his main theologian had the right to propound such principles; but such affirmations may also be incendiary in the political arena. John Paul II and Joseph Ratzinger recognized this last point.

The Preferential Option for the Poor

These principles turned revolutionary in 1968, when the Latin American bishops met at Medellín in Columbia and resolved to proclaim a "preferential option for the poor," going so far as to acknowledge that those "who set their hopes on violence, in view of the gravity of the injustice and of the illegitimate resistance to a change in society, are frequently motivated in the last analysis by noble ideas of justice and solidarity."

Since that time, the mighty in Latin America have continued to put up a harsh resistance to Christian demands for justice. Those in the ranks of the clergy who endeavored to improve the living conditions of the faithful were dismissed as Marxist, socialist, or a threat to state security, and this resistance was a significant reason why a number of priests did in fact become revolutionaries: those who spoke out on behalf of a better life for the poor became apostles of the salvation to be sought in communism. Confronted with the sheer misery of the masses, their social involvement did not always stick to tried and trusted paths. It proved exceedingly hard, if not indeed impossible, to persuade the powerful, the rich, and the well-fed to accept the spirit of Christian solidarity; those who were well-off may have thought "the raising up of the lowly and the feeding of the hungry" to be a mere utopia in present-day circumstances, or perhaps in any social system whatever.

If liberation theology had lost some of its power to convince, fifteen years after Medellín, this was not—as its zealous spokesmen maintained—because it had been continuously persecuted by conservative bishops and those who had political power. The reasons were more complex, and it was at this point that Cardinal Ratzinger took action. The Latin American bishops as a whole began to reflect on the possibilities of political intervention on the part of the church, and more and more bishops took the view that the status quo was the lesser evil, even when governments were decreasing their commitment to the liberation of the people from misery, ignorance, and exploitation, and necessary reform measures were dying on the vine. The violence employed in the struggle for liberation in some Latin American countries usually claimed even more victims among the people and caused more oppression than an imperfect form of government. Revolution was not a clean stroke of the surgeon's knife to cut off the evil head of a violent society.

Catholic theologians, including the International Theological Commission in the Vatican and the former Jesuit general Pedro Arrupe, were identifying with increasing clarity those instances where liberation theology had fallen into the snares of Marxism, once it took the leap from the religious sphere into the harsh realities of daily life; and priests sought to make their proclamation of the kingdom of God a recipe for improvements here on earth. The church could not accept Marxism, which was an atheistic and wholly worldly doctrine of salvation.

In some countries, the bishops also noted that incautious liberation theologians and priests who took up the cause of social justice were being drawn into conflicts between political parties, so that the timelessness of their mission was sullied with the hatred of political controversies. In some places, a "church of the people" came into existence; its representatives thought that they could act in a kind of political vacuum, but they were accused of letting themselves be used by political forces as an instrument against other Catholics and against the bishops. The refusal of John Paul II to accept a "church of the people" cut adrift from the church of the episcopal hierarchy, his refusal to allow religious and priests to be political activists, his declarations against the reduction of the Christian message to a welfare program, and his condemnations of Marxism and communism became ever clearer.

Does this mean that Cardinal Ratzinger, obedient to the orders of the pope, had slain the dragon of liberation theology once and for all? No, because the commitment of the church to help the poor was not affected by the verdict pronounced on liberation theology as a political program. Freedom and liberation remained central ideas of the Christianity that is lived by the Catholic Church in Latin America, just as in other regions. But the Vatican had stripped the liberation theologians of their political innocence. Joseph Ratzinger, the guardian of the faith, wanted them to work as a leaven among Catholics for the amelioration of social conditions, not to be the colleagues of partisans and guerrillas.

A worthwhile desire on Ratzinger's part, but not a popular one.

Another Phone Call

First there came a phone call from Munich. All I heard in the beginning was a persistent rumor. It was not so easy to believe the official denials of this rumor, for I myself heard in the corridors of the Vatican that the pope was looking for someone to head the Congregation for the Doctrine of the Faith. The Croatian cardinal Franjo Šeper became prefect in 1968, three years after the Council, and remained in office until his death in 1981. He was a reliable and cautious theologian but hardly brilliant. Nevertheless, John Paul II praised him at his Requiem on January 2, 1982: "In an extremely difficult period, he was the prudent and enlightened leader of this Congregation, which was obliged to intervene on decisive questions concerning faith and morals." By then, he had already appointed Šeper's successor, the cardinal archbishop of Munich. The Vatican believed that he too was "prudent and enlightened."

I received a second phone call, this time from a colleague in Frankfurt who had called me earlier after the first promotion of Joseph Ratzinger from university professor to archbishop in Munich, and had said—with reference to my first article about Ratzinger—"That's how people get promoted!" He repeated the same words this time, and added: "Just keep up the good work! We'll see what becomes of Ratzinger!" I was a little uneasy about the idea of a German as Grand Inquisitor in Rome, but I was happy to think I would soon meet an old acquaintance again.

At Home in the Catholic World

My life as a child and a young man, my education, my relations with my family: all this helped me to understand him, although he was older and had a very different life from my own. I could understand his background, his studies, and his intellectual ambitions; I could understand why he was so much

19

at home in the Catholic world, for we had the same basically good experience of this world. He was born in 1927, and his autobiography, *Milestones* (1997, English translation 1998), gives a good insight into the intact world of Bavarian Catholicism when he was a child and a young man. These memoirs cover the first fifty years of his life, a subject about which he has often spoken with me. His family opposed the Nazi regime (1933–1945), which posed an ominous threat from his sixth to his eighteenth year. He automatically joined the Hitler Youth and worked as an air-raid helper toward the end of the war: resistance on his part would have been completely pointless and might have meant a death sentence. Inner resistance was another matter altogether. . . .

I once told him that some years later, probably in 1952 or 1953, I was living in East Berlin in communist East Germany, where I experienced something similar. I was to be "enrolled" in the Young Pioneers, the communist youth organization. My parents objected, saying that "enough care is being taken of the young man," but pressure from my school became so unpleasantly harsh that my father decided to flee from the Soviet sector of Berlin and to bring his family to live in freedom in the American and English sectors of the city, which were only a few miles away. This meant that I did not have to wear the blue neckerchief of the Young Pioneers; instead, I found my home in the Catholic Youth Association. It was impossible for the Ratzinger family to flee from Hitler's Third Reich, but the Catholic world provided a place of refuge. This remained true after the war, when Germany was in ruins.

Ratzinger's experiences of feasts and celebrations and of the daily customs that accompanied people's lives from the cradle to the grave were all Catholic, and they did him good. His studies of philosophy and theology, which culminated in his ordination to the priesthood on June 19, 1951, opened up wide spaces of freedom and gave him the glimpse of a higher life, after the political catastrophe during his early years. I knew what this must have meant to him, since I grew up in the Catholic diaspora of "godless" postwar Berlin, where I experienced my Catholic life in a somewhat colorless society as richer and more colorful than the lives of others with whom I came into contact. I did not feel that my life was hampered by Catholic regulations or prohibitions.

One almost hesitates, in view of today's universal demand for sharp criticism, to talk about this basic contentment with the Catholic Church! But that is how Joseph Ratzinger has always felt, and it may have prevented him from feeling empathy with those who did not share this basic feeling of contentment. I at any rate could grasp how the newly appointed prefect would go about his work, although I had taken a very different path after my studies of philosophy and theology at the Pontifical Gregorian University in Rome from 1963 to 1970/1973. Learned Jesuits had emphatically shown me there what was Catholic and what was not, what one may contemplate in the wide spaces of those questions that have not yet been officially settled, what was an open question and what was not. Perhaps these wise priests, who were drawn from all over the world, and the contacts with students of theology from so many different countries taught me that it is truly Catholic to acknowledge principles in a quite natural manner, without a rebellious protest, just as it is necessary to reckon with the possibility of deviations from these principles in practice—what the moral theologians call sin. One could thus say that I had good presuppositions for a dialogue with the prefect, without getting into conflicts with him.

Meeting Mozart in Heaven

We did not talk so much about his work and the theological subjects directly connected with it, for we did not need to hold a learned debate, nor did we wish to do so—we were both familiar with all the relevant arguments and could take for granted that we didn't need to remind each other of them. I knew Joseph Ratzinger's books and articles, and he (although he read only the Bavarian newspapers) knew my journalistic work. It was therefore not a case of finding better arguments but of looking at different assessments and different perspectives, and examining the importance to be attributed to the individual arguments. He was a church theologian who looked with a critical eye at the developments in his church and attempted to steer these with intellectual acuteness and clarity; I was a "secular" journalist in a mainstream newspaper, obliged every day by developments in society and my experience of politics and politicians to get involved with the church and its leaders. And I felt that the church would not profit from taking exactly the same path in society that we had already seen.

At the same time, I got to know Joseph Ratzinger better, as a priest of credibility, an authentically spiritual man, a modest person, whose life was nourished by the Christian faith, celebrating Mass every day, praying the psalms in the Divine Office, which Catholic priests are required to pray daily, and often saying the rosary with its repetitions of the Lord's Prayer, the Ave Maria, and the Glory Be to the Father. He also meditated on sacred scripture, especially on the Gospels with their challenging narratives and their wonderfully apt parables. It was per-

Joseph Ratzinger was born in the nearly 300-year-old "Customs House" on the Market Square in Marktl (photograph taken 1920).

wr, Marktl	1 10 p.m.	1 50 p.m.		Kirchfüllen.	
Marktl	14. April 3 h p.m.	16. April 8 30 a.m.	J. Stangl Coop.	Anna Engl Grubbsitzerin Marktl	
Marktl	16. April 4 15 a.m.	16. April 8 30 a.m.	J. Stangl Coop.	Anna Ratzinger	Kröstu Achum Rotphirsch,
München–Freising ernannt, 28. Mai 1974 Bischofsweihe in München,					
Marktl	21. April 11 45 a.m.	22. April 8 h a.m.	J. Stangl Coop.	Maria Liergraber Grübsitzgattin Marktl	27. Juni 1977 Kardinal
Marktl	21. April 10 30 a.m.	22. April 1 h p.m.	J. Stangl Coop.	Dina Meier Freihauergattin Marktl	

Entry in the baptismal register, Marktl.

The church in Marktl am Inn, birthplace of Joseph Ratzinger

The font in which Joseph Ratzinger was baptized, now in the local museum in Marktl.

Joseph Ratzinger in the uniform of a German military anti-aircraft unit helper (1943).

Lecturer in dogmatics and fundamental theology in Freising (summer semester 1955).

The Ratzinger family after the first Masses of the two brothers, July 8, 1951.

The Ratzinger family before the departure from Freising (spring, 1959). From l. to r.: Joseph (son), Maria (mother), Joseph (father), Maria (sister), Georg.

Mass on a mountain near Ruhpolding (summer 1952).

Joseph Ratzinger in conversation with Yves Congar during the Second Vatican Council.

Meeting between
Cardinal Ratzinger and
Ruth Stapleton-Carter,
sister of President Jimmy
Carter, during her
five-day visit to Germany,
September 29, 1977
(Munich).

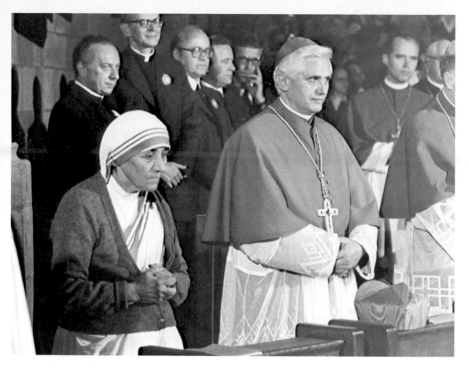

85th German "Catholic Day" in Freiburg, September 13-17, 1978: Mother Teresa and Cardinal Ratzinger.

Cardinal Ratzinger receives the Mayor of Jerusalem, Teddy Kollek, in the Catholic Academy, Munich, July 9, 1980.

Cardinal Ratzinger receives Patrick Chakaipa, Archbishop of Harare/Zimbabwe, May 21, 1978.

Meeting of the Protestant Academy in Tutzing, April 27, 1979: the Russian Orthodox Archbishop of Sagorsk, Vladimir Dimitrovsky, and Cardinal Ratzinger.

Joseph Ratzinger, professor for Catholic dogmatics at the University of Regensburg, during the fourth session of Vatican II, September 14, 1965.

About 7,500 persons, including Cardinal Ratzinger, the Bavarian prime minister Franz Josef Strauss, and the minister for culture Hans Maier, take part in a demonstration in Munich on December 21, 1981, demanding the immediate release of thousands of political prisoners from internment in Poland.

85th German "Catholic Day" in Freiburg, September 13-17, 1978: Cardinal Ratzinger in Freiburg cathedral.

Conclusion of the celebrations of the Augsburg Confession, Augsburg, June 20, 1980: from l., Federal President Karl Carstens; Cardinal Jan Willebrands, President of the Vatican Secretariat for Christian Unity; Cardinal Ratzinger; G. Heintze, Protestant bishop in Brunswick; Greek Orthodox Metropolitan Irenaeus.

Joint Commission of the Council of the Protestant Church in Germany and the German Bishops' Conference, May 6-7, 1981, in Munich. From r.: Hermann Cardinal Volk (Mainz); Bishop Eduard Lohse, President of the Council of the Protestant Church; Bishop Martin Kruse; Bishop Paul Werner Scheele.

Cardinal Ratzinger in Czestochowa, September 1980

Archbishop Joseph Ratzinger playing piano.

fectly obvious that his thinking was at home in this world of faith. This made the church's feasts not only religious high points but days that must be marked on a human level too. He took great care in the celebration of his patron, Saint Joseph, on March 19 each year, inviting other Josephs whom he knew in Rome to join in Mass or on a well-planned excursion to the countryside outside the city.

When I collected him on a Sunday from his apartment outside the Vatican walls, in the Piazza della Città Leonina, to bring him to lunch in our apartment, he always had a gift with him— something special which showed that he had given the matter thought, something that would give his hosts pleasure. One day, for example, he proudly presented us with the newest CD of music by the "Regensburg Domspatzen" (literally, the "cathedral sparrows") "who are directed by my famous brother, Georg Ratzinger." He talked about his brother and said that he was worried for one reason and another; and he talked about his sister, Maria, who was his housekeeper and did not feel truly at home in Rome, because the Romans were so un-Bavarian. The cardinal regretted that he did not have enough time to be with her. He would like to go more often with her to the Campo Santo, the small, peaceful German cemetery alongside the Collegio Teutonico, a quiet place in the shadows of Saint Peter's Basilica where they would sit and talk about the old days, about their beloved parents—"Do you remember . . . ?" They enjoyed remembering familiar places and events; they looked at the cats who played among the tombstones, and relaxed.

The cardinal appreciated music. He is one of those theologians, like the great Protestant Karl Barth, who look forward to heaven because they will meet Johann Sebastian Bach, Wolfgang Amadeus Mozart, and Anton Bruckner there. If there is one privilege connected with his new office of which Benedict XVI would gladly avail himself, it would be to have more contact with the great composers.

Not all the popes have been as musical as Benedict XVI! One evening, shortly after Christmas, his faithful secretary, Josef Clemens (now a bishop in the Pontifical Council for the Laity) drove him home, exhausted after a long and strenuous day in his office. The cardinal revived at once when Clemens mentioned a new electronic piano: "Where.is the instrument? Where is it?" And when he began to play, all his weariness vanished.

He gladly made presents of costly bottles of spirits that people had given him, for he very seldom drank alcohol—a glass of beer occasionally, a glass of champagne or bubbling white wine on a feast day. Choice wines meant little to him. Once, he brought us two bottles of an old, select port wine from a famous Portuguese firm, vintage 1970. I opened one of them on a special occasion—was it when he was elected dean of the College of Cardinals in November 2002?

I still have the second one, now covered in dust. I cannot quite make up my mind whether I should open it.

The Good Health of the Church

Cardinal Ratzinger went on to lose more friends inside and outside the Catholic Church. In an interview, he used the word "restoration" to sum up what ought to happen to the church now. In Europe, this concept is laden with heavy political baggage. The history of the nineteenth century is still perceived in such negative terms that not even the positive use of the word—for example, when we speak of the restoration of old houses—

can help the elegant Latin word *restaurare* sound good in our ears. Accordingly, the German cardinal was obliged to follow up the first interview in the Italian periodical *Jesus* with a second interview in *Trenta Giorni* (*Thirty Days*) in which he offered an explanation and clarification of his earlier remarks. Not a few in the Vatican held the opinion that the head of one of its departments shouldn't give interviews at all, and even cardinals in Rome were heard to observe, with a touch of malice, that their German colleague "talks too much." Naturally, I didn't agree with this—for I wanted to know what Ratzinger planned for the church under the powerful figure of John Paul II.

I already knew Joseph Ratzinger as professor in Regensburg and as Archbishop in Munich, so it was not possible for me to evaluate his most recent affirmations on the level of offensive slogans. They had to be understood as an illustration of the way he was currently thinking—and that was interesting, for it could shed new light on the concept of restoration as the "recovery of lost values in the framework of a new totality." Naturally, there was some way to go before I reached this illumination. . . .

One aspect inherent in the office Ratzinger held was that he didn't speak primarily about the good health of the church. A historian would surely find it easy to demonstrate that the Roman Catholic Church with the pope at its head had reached a high point in its development, historically speaking, in the 1950s, and once again in the 1980s; just try to think of one century that today's bishops would choose in preference to our own epoch! But the office of prefect of the Congregation for the Doctrine of the Faith involves examining the life of faith in the church to detect the first symptoms of sickness, the first pointers to a potential problem, or the first consequences of a disturbance that has actually occurred.

The word "crisis" plays a key role in Ratzinger's "Analysis of the Contemporary Situation of the Faith," which was later published in the Vatican newspaper *L'Osservatore Romano*. Even I found it hard to decide whether the cardinal was simply yielding here to the intellectual skepticism of his own personality or following the fashionable trend of those who are quite incapable of saying anything about politics and economics, culture and religion, without employing the word "crisis."

I am, after all, a secular journalist; I do not write for a church newspaper. And so I thought that perhaps Cardinal Ratzinger's high position in the Vatican had led him, like many other bishops, to regret that the church and the world are not identical, to find it a pity that society is not a monastery, and the monastery not society. On the other hand, one must bear in mind the theological question whether the fullness of God's creation and human life could be led *only* behind walls set up by the narrowness of ecclesiastical regulations. For outside those walls, outside the solid defenses of the church's fortress, believers and unbelievers lived together, and cultures developed in a thousand forms, good and bad, without first waiting to hear a verdict pronounced on them by the church. The "autonomy of worldly affairs" had progressed without the church.

Prescribing Strong Medicine

I continued my journalistic thoughts; I am accustomed to take a critical view of normal matters and persons in society, since I am conscious of their imperfection. Perhaps it would be worthwhile for the Christian and non-Christian alike to taste the bitter medicine offered by Ratzinger, who is after all a highly educated theologian and a prudent physician of the faith. Perhaps a critical self-examination would do us all some good. How about these words of the cardinal?

> In a world where skepticism has infected even Christian believers, people are offended by the church's conviction that there is a truth that can be precisely defined and expressed. The church is not merely a human organization, and must therefore defend a deposit, a treasure of faith, which does not belong to the church, but comes from God.

Ratzinger had this to say about the Second Vatican Council:

> I believe that the Council cannot actually be held to account for false developments and false forms. On the contrary, these contradict both the spirit and the letter of its documents. Those who yearn for the Council of Trent or the First Vatican Council, just like those who consider those two councils obsolete, forget that all three councils are upheld by precisely the same authority: by the college of bishops in union with the pope.

Nevertheless, Ratzinger pointed out "damage." Inside the church, "hidden, aggressive, polemic, separatist, perhaps irresponsible powers have been unleashed." In Western society, we see "the upper middle class of the tertiary-sector bourgeoisie establishing itself, with its radical liberal ideology, which is individualistic, rationalistic, and hedonistic." Strong words!

In this summary in the *Osservatore*, Ratzinger went on to define the crisis of faith as he had done in our own previous conversations. One must differentiate among the various worlds and cultures. In Latin America, there was a risk that the church could fall under the spell of Marxist promises. In the First World, it risks disfigurement by a libertine, liberal, radical culture that would detach it from Christian morality: "A culture is devilish when it succeeds in convincing people that the only goal for their lives is pleasure and their own private interests." In Europe, theologians had to speak of a "world that is disenchanted, a world now grown old, tormented by academic arrogance and a coldness that is impervious to emotion."

Other difficulties were present in North America: "Wealth as the criterion of life; difficulties with authentic Catholic morality, which is often expressed in the alternatives of dissent from society, or dissent from the magisterium. In Africa and Asia, inculturation and ecumenism pose difficulties." The result of his analysis of the East seemed paradoxical: "Faith seems to be most sure precisely where it is persecuted." He summed up as follows: there is a risk "that we may fall for the immanentist position proposed in the programs of secularist liberation. If we seek the truth of Christianity only in the natural sphere, and not in the supernatural sphere too, we deprive the faith of its original promise and mutilate the human person, whose specific characteristic it is to overcome nature."

A bitter medicine. But helpful medicines are often bitter.

A Cardinal in Dialogue

On Monday, November 25, 1985, a gray, cold November morning in Rome, the "Extraordinary Synod of the Bishops of the Catholic Church" began. Exactly four years earlier, on November 25, 1981, the pope had appointed Archbishop Joseph Ratzinger to head the CDF. John Paul II had convened this "miniature council" in order to hear from the representatives of the national episcopal conferences and from the most important Vatican prelates. How would they assess the situation of the church twenty years after the close of the Second Vatican Council (1962–1965)? It was not Ratzinger's intention to celebrate his four years in the new office. In the Catholic calendar, that day was the feast of Catherine of Alexandria, one of the saints known as the Fourteen Auxiliaries.

Nevertheless, the synod was dominated by the German curial cardinal, the fifty-eight-year-old former professor of theology who had become very influential behind the walls of the Vatican and in the world church. The only thing uncertain was whether bishops from such a great variety of countries would accept or reject the theological and ecclesial-political guidelines laid down by the prefect of the CDF. They might make them even more rigid—or they might tone them down. Would the synod learn from Ratzinger? Would Ratzinger learn from the synod? Or both from each other?

Indeed, the prefect had become a well-known figure in the universal church and in Rome's church circles. In his daily work, he usually wore a black suit with a clerical collar in the Roman style; he donned the formal uniform of a prince of the church only when etiquette dictated. He made a friendly impression— the kind of friendliness that is appropriate when one meets everyday people, such as pilgrims from his Bavarian homeland. This was part of the professional attitude of a pastor, one might say, especially when he was a bishop. But the Bavarian could become very cool when he felt challenged in a debate about issues, for then it was primarily the abstract arguments that his razor-sharp intellect perceived, and the dialogue with a partner could easily turn into an unemotional analysis. This accusation had occasionally been leveled at him during his time as archbishop in Munich.

If the cardinal found his dialogue partner not too far below him intellectually, he united his exceptional keenness of mind with a personal warmth in a manner that was both impressive and charming. His affirmations had a certainty that some people called (and continue to call) intellectual arrogance, but even if that were the case, there were extenuating circumstances. The Catholic Church had always spoiled Joseph Ratzinger, as it were. It educated him, made him important, and gave him space for growth in a way paralleled only by a life such as that of Julius Döpfner, Ratzinger's predecessor as archbishop of Munich, who became bishop in Würzburg at the age of thirty-five, and, at age forty-five, the youngest cardinal in the church. While Döpfner experienced tense times with the church, Ratzinger seemed to enjoy perfect harmony with regard to everything Catholic.

The participants in the synod knew that Joseph Ratzinger became professor of theology in Freising near Munich at the age of thirty-one. Ratzinger had a lightning career, although he had never been ambitious in this sense.

Naturally, the synod fathers also knew of the celebrated speech during the Council in which the blind Cardinal Frings accused the Holy Office under Cardinal Alfredo Ottaviani—today's CDF—of a whole list of sins. A sigh of relief went through Saint Peter's Basilica on that occasion. Joseph Ratzinger had helped write that speech, and it is an irony of history that it was Cardinal Ratzinger who later had to deliver on the promises made by the theologian he was then. And despite all the nonsensical chatter, he was in fact attempting to make good on those promises in the hands-on leadership of the CDF. But what did the prefect think about all that happened in (and to) the Catholic Church during the four years of the Second Vatican Council, from 1962 to 1965?

Many Catholics and other Christians were extraordinarily unsure about how to evaluate the events of that period, which will continue to influence the church for many years. Embittered debates have erupted about whether the "crises" in the church—the decline of numbers attending Mass, of priests, and of women religious—are the effect of the Council, or whether everything would just have been much worse if there had been no Council at all. Many would love to return to the period before the Council, to the "Pian epoch," which ran from Pius VI (1775–1799) to Pius XII (1939–1958). Many would love to rewrite the conciliar texts.

Many complain that the Second Vatican Council has been "badly studied, badly interpreted, and badly implemented," as John Paul II himself said in a discourse in Belgium early in 1985. For others again, the Council "did not go far enough." They smell treason everywhere and fear a relapse into the Dark Ages, as soon as they hear anyone speak of the "spirit of the Council" in anything other than laudatory tones.

Cultural Ferment and the Faith

Ratzinger took a different view. His experiences with students as a professor and his experiences with committed lay Catholics at the Common Synod of the Dioceses in the Federal Republic of Germany (1971 to 1975 in Würzburg) taught him a different lesson. The Ariadne's thread running through the labyrinth of Ratzinger's thought is the insight that dramatic changes have occurred in the "world," that is, in society; the liberal spirit of the Western world is in a profound crisis, a crisis proclaimed on the barricades in Paris in the student uprisings in May, 1968. "Opening up" and "aggiornamento" are slogans that have created a vacuum in educated Catholics, thanks to an opening up and an accommodation of the church vis-à-vis the world. The spiritual elites of the church, in the university lecture halls and in religious orders such as the Jesuits, have lost many members. The identity of Catholicism had become nebulous, and this must be rediscovered and affirmed with clarity.

This does not mean that the professor wanted to reject the Council. He wanted to bid farewell to the illusions of his younger self: the illusion that the Council will allow the Catholic Church to win over the world, the other Christian churches, and the great Eastern religions (given a little good will); the illusion that after the "bastions were overthrown" (in the prophetic title of a book published by the Swiss theologian Hans Urs von Balthasar in 1952), humanity would stream into the bosom of the church; the fallacy that the openness of the men and women of the church would lead humanity to enter voluntarily the closed "monastery" of pious faith.

Ratzinger insisted in his writings and lectures that the revolutions that shook the church at that time were only the equivalent of what was going on elsewhere in the world: intellectual ferments in the Western democracies, which erupted in the student protests and led to new political constellations; revisionist processes in the communist states, which were advancing slowly and almost imperceptibly; in the Third World, the breakthrough of the peoples to achieve independence from the colonial powers and self-determination. This means that it is a mere academic exercise to debate the meaning and outcome of the Council for the church. It happened. It belongs to history. It brought insights that cannot be extinguished.

And this is why Ratzinger has consistently rejected all attempts to get rid of the Council by means of a restoration. In *The Ratzinger Report* (published in 1985), for example, he affirms: "If 'restoration' means going back, then no kind of restoration is possible. The church marches forward to the fulfillment of history. No, one does not go back, nor can one." He sees the church's main task as the "search for a new equilibrium, after all the exaggerations of an undiscriminating opening to the world, after the excessively positive interpretations of a world that is agnostic and atheistic." The goal is a "newly discovered balance of orientations and values within Catholicism as a whole."

Shouldering a Heavy Burden

During his time as archbishop of Munich (1977–1981), the former professor of theology had new experiences of the church and the world. First of all, there was the fact that the pope expected great things of him, as did the Catholics in Munich. Nevertheless, many were not happy with him, thinking that he had been promoted too quickly. Many were impressed by the edifying homilies of the cardinal archbishop, and by his skill at speaking, his ability to tackle even sensitive subjects. When he stood in the pulpit, he fascinated the faithful, but his well-chosen words lost much of their luster when they returned to their daily lives. In Munich, he came to realize that the relationship between church and world is not a matter of two abstract entities but of the individual believer. He saw things now in a larger perspective: in the Council, the church did set out to conquer the world, incurring rejection and painful wounds in the process; but this was not all we should have been doing: the church ought to have created a harmony for Catholics themselves between finding a home in the church and the experience of being foreigners in the world, between Sunday and weekday work, between faith and reason, and between ecclesiastical tradition and modern culture.

He realized that the faithful—just like those who were rather less faithful—often bore within themselves a large portion of world and a small portion of church. And he realized that, in most people's lives, the question of the theoretical truth of the faith and of the lifeless correctness of a moral doctrine never in fact gets asked.

The archbishop was snatched out of his learning process in Munich. John Paul II wanted to have him beside him in Rome because he believed that Ratzinger had the ability to take an overview of the whole of Catholic doctrine and to issue both specific warnings against deviations and helpful guidelines about what the true faith was. A heavy burden was thus laid on the shoulders of the German cardinal. In Western history, the "Congregation for the Doctrine of the Faith" (the word "Sacred" had been dropped in recent editions of the Vatican Yearbook) holds an ambiguous place. Both to the Enlightenment's pursuit of perfect reason and to the gentle spirit of the gospels, the idea of such a guardian institution seems offensive. Therefore, it was not only the challenges of the future but specific burdens of the past as well that Ratzinger had to face in his new position.

The Long Shadow of History

How to makes sense of the CDF's existence and controversial history? An appeal to Saint Paul's words in the First Letter to the Corinthians that divisions and heresies in the church are inevitable, "in order that it may be clearly seen who among you are approved (in the faith)," does not seem helpful today. Nor does the assertion that Catholic understanding requires that there be a body in the church that can carry out the discernment of spirits. It is just as little helpful to recall that the Christian emperors in antiquity, a Theodosius in the fourth century and a Justinian, imposed on heretics and schismatics the penalties of confiscation of their goods, exile, and death. Or that the German emperor Frederick Barbarossa organized the struggle against every form of heresy at the synod of Verona in 1184 and threatened to outlaw heretics and their sympathizers. Or that it was believed in the thirteenth century that the only way to preserve the unity of the faith—which was identical to the unity of the political cosmos—was by setting up an Inquisition in order to defend the church against the religious sects that were popping up like mushrooms all over the place.

This view was taken not only in the dark Middle Ages, nor only by the madness of the obsession that Spaniards felt at the end of the fifteenth century about those Jews and Muslims whose conversion to Catholicism was only a matter of outward appearances. The sixteenth-century Reformers likewise declared the persecution of deviant professions of faith to be a useful instrument in the protection of the faith. It was at this period, in 1542 (two years after the foundation of the Jesuit order), that Paul III, known to art historians for the beautiful

buildings he erected in Rome, founded the "Sacred Congregation of the Universal Inquisition." His explicit intention was to
defend the church against heresy, and especially against Protes-
tantism. This body was so much feared that people were reluctant to call it by its real name: they spoke instead of the "Holy
Office."

The shadows of the past clustered around the prefect. El
Greco, the Greek-Spanish artist, painted Cardinal Nino de
Guevara, "Grand Inquisitor" in Spain and archbishop of Seville,
around 1600, the year in which the philosopher Giordano
Bruno was burned at the stake on the Campo de' Fiori in Rome
after condemnation by the Roman Inquisition. And we also see
the dramatic form of the Grand Inquisitor, a churchman bowed
by age, in the Russian author Dostoevsky's *Brothers Karamazov*.

Famous Instructions

When Joseph Ratzinger published some clarifying theological ideas under the harmless (and precise) title "Instruction on
Some Aspects of the Theology of Liberation" in September
1984, he unleashed a storm. He immediately lost favor with
those who read his differentiated criticism of specific points of
liberation theology as a general attack on every endeavor to
achieve social justice in Third World countries. He also lost
favor with those who were well disposed to Marxism and social-
ism, for Ratzinger delivered an onslaught on these ideologies
too. Finally, he provoked the entire communist world to fury
when he called it "the shame of our time" and dismissed its
favorite concepts, "revolution" and "class struggle," as an "illusion." Until that time, the prefect of the CDF had been

respected by most of these groups, but now he came to experience in a personally painful way how much influence they had on public opinion. It was not even a matter of taking his arguments seriously and refuting him; there were few at that time who thought him worthy of a measured response at all.

The German cardinal did something else: he met one of the representatives of liberation theology, the Brazilian Franciscan Leonardo Boff, for a conversation, and delivered a theological verdict on him some months later. He thereby aroused the opposition of some of the Brazilian bishops and of many people in Latin America. The Franciscans and many from other religious orders joined in the chorus of protest, for they saw the proceedings taken against Leonardo Boff as a disciplinary measure of the Vatican directed against the religious communities in general. But this was not all. The Belgian curial Cardinal Hamer, the authoritarian prefect of the Congregation for the Religious Orders, insisted that a period of penitential silence be imposed on the Brazilian Franciscan, and Ratzinger finally agreed to this. This provoked a furious reaction on the part of some Catholics and others, and the prefect increasingly came to be seen as the embodiment of a reactionary course in the church, which was taking a direction away from the freedoms of the Council.

In a sense, Ratzinger himself provided fuel for this interpretation, when he had a conversation with the Italian journalist Vittorio Messori (*The Ratzinger Report*, mentioned earlier). This text would not have been out of place as a contribution to a discussion in academic circles, and that is in fact its original intention. But it was possible to misunderstand it as an authoritative declaration of the church's political goals pursued in the pontificate of John Paul II. What Ratzinger actually says in this book-long interview is neither particularly exciting nor altogether original, and yet it raises question marks in the reader's mind precisely because it comes with the seal of the authority of the prefect of the CDF. And the reader may wonder: if, as we noted earlier, Ratzinger thinks it so important to look for a new equilibrium in the church, then his primary obligation is surely to establish this unity—not to take up a position on one side of the ecclesial debate.

Joseph Ratzinger, however, is a man of the abstract truth. The first thing his eyes see is the academic disputation, and this reveals his "innocence" in church politics. Ratzinger is no *homo politicus*. If he were, how could he possibly deliver a sharp attack in his lengthy interview on the institution of the episcopal conferences, with which he was constantly in touch? In church politics, his keen intelligence sometimes lets him down.

If this were not the case, he would not have asserted that the national episcopal conferences lack a theological basis. For in saying this, he played down the ancient Catholic tradition of the "metropolitan" associations, that is, several dioceses hierarchically bound to a strong archdiocese, in favor of the centralizing demands issued by Rome. Was he not afraid that the same theological logic might be applied to call into question the justification of the statements made by the CDF? Might one not say that his Congregation was merely articulating an exaggerated tendency to claim that papal infallibility (in which Catholics must believe) extends to each and every area in which—according to the traditional teaching—the pope is not in fact infallible?

At this point, however, the theological master in Joseph Ratzinger would step in and declare without hesitation that he was not and is not infallible; nor can his be the final word. Then one could take up a dialogue with him, and he would listen to one's analyses of the situation of the church decades after the end of the Council and of the path it should now take. He could then be convinced by other relevant arguments that would lead to a better conclusion.

At that synod in 1985, the bishops of the worldwide church were invited to speak in Rome. Oddly enough, I do not recall much of what they said.

There He Stands

Twelve years later, as I prepared to join Joseph Ratzinger to celebrate his seventieth birthday, things had not changed.

At that time, people were prone to wax eloquent about his role in the church and the extent of his influence. As a German living in Rome, I got tired of hearing the same words over and over again. Whether it was cardinals and archbishops in the Roman curia or the bishops from every country in the world who came for their *ad limina* visit "to the thresholds" of the tombs of the apostles Peter and Paul in Rome, where they gave an account of their episcopal ministry to the papal congregations and councils, all agreed, whether in public press conferences or in confidential conversations, that no German since Martin Luther had made such a powerful impression on the form and substance of the Catholic Church as Joseph Ratzinger.

Luther lived in the sixteenth century, a long time ago; many churches and ecclesial communities are proud to claim him as their spiritual father. He died in Eisleben on February 18, 1546, and the many commemorative addresses and celebrations in 1996, four hundred and fifty years later, recalled the historical importance of the Reformer, the "German par excellence."

Ratzinger is not a rebel from central Germany like Luther, but an Upper Bavarian from the region of the river Inn. The fact that the Marian pilgrimage town of Altötting is not far from Marktl, Ratzinger's birthplace, does not necessarily mean that everyone who lives there is a good, pious, and unquestioning Catholic, but that was true of Joseph Ratzinger. For seventy years, he had been a faithful son of his church and one of the fixed stars in the theological constellation for nearly forty years. Since his appointment as prefect of the CDF in 1981, he had been nothing less than the North Star of the largest Christian community of faith. It is he who drew the coordinates of the doctrine of the faith, although (or perhaps precisely because) he was answerable to John Paul II, a very strong pope.

The CDF was founded in 1542, only a few years before Luther's death, as the "Sacred Congregation of the Universal Inquisition," and it acquired a dubious reputation as the "Holy Office."

The Grand Inquisitors left their mark on the history of European and Western culture not so much through their person as through their work—with a few exceptions, such as Thomas de Torquemada at the end of the fifteenth century. He intervened in the course of Spanish and world history as the father confessor of Isabella the Catholic and Ferdinand of Aragon, the sovereigns remembered for sending out Christopher Columbus on his voyage and oppressing Muslims and Jews.

A man like Galileo Galilei is more famous than his judges in the church's Inquisition; similarly, the "Index of Forbidden Books" is more famous than those who compiled it (and abolished it in 1966). History tends to forget the prefect of the CDF. But Ratzinger is not so easily forgotten.

It was a cliché even then to suggest that "the young progressive simply turned into an old reactionary." This did not suffice to explain his global influence alongside the increasingly ailing pope. If one wishes to be fair to Ratzinger—and there were people who did not wish this—and to do justice to what has actually happened in the Catholic Church in the last several decades, one must probe more deeply. The death of Pius XII on October 9, 1958, and the election of John XXIII three weeks later marked the beginning of a new epoch. The cultural revolution, the existential crisis of a Eurocentric church, of which the Second Vatican Council (1962–1965) is certainly a part and an expression, and Ratzinger's task as prefect of the CDF can best be illuminated by means of a precise and comprehensive Latin aphorism of Pope Clement XIII. Clement, who reigned from 1758 to 1769, in the age of the Enlightenment and freemasonry, refused the demand of the French government to "nationalize" the French Jesuits. In his memorable words, *Aut sint ut sunt aut non sint* ("Let them be as they are [that is, oriented to the universal papal church], or else let them not exist at all").

These words can be applied to the church itself: *aut sit ut est aut non sit*. "Let the church be what it is, or else let it not exist at all." This has been the overarching theological motto of both the young and the old Joseph Ratzinger, both in the conciliar period when the primary task was to rediscover what the church and Catholicism were, and at the beginning of the third millennium, where (rightly or wrongly) Rome led the resistance to what the church and Catholicism ought not to be.

Ratzinger would add another clause: *aut non erit*, "or else it will not exist." This seems to have been the conclusion that he drew, and it was held as a maxim in the apostolic palace of the pope . . . and many bishops would say that this applied not only to John Paul II but to whomever will be the pope after him, including Benedict XVI.

A Joyful Confidence

Because the stakes were so high for such a long time, I always found it stimulating to interact with Joseph Ratzinger. Over the years, I spent many hours talking with him, and he always had something valuable to say. As much today in the first days of his papacy as in his earlier days as a theologian, he knows how to kindle enthusiasm, to win assent, to provoke objections and contrary arguments; he always succeeds in making me reflect. If I can say that I have sometimes glimpsed the unbending harshness of the Grand Inquisitor, it was in his allergy against all the folly that is spread abroad in the church and the world. Ratzinger saw through everything that was stupid, even before he put the question about orthodoxy or set out the criteria for discerning correct doctrine. One might say that Ratzinger added a somewhat astonishing clause to the ancient wisdom propounded by scholastic philosophy in the Middle Ages, that that which is, is one and true and good. Ratzinger said that that which is Catholic cannot be stupid, and that which is stupid cannot be Catholic. Before the head of the Holy Office sniffed out and identified a heresy or something contrary to the faith, I sometimes had the impression that he instinctively shrank back from the stupidity that such ideas contained. This reminded me of the English writer G. K. Chesterton, who expressed a similar confidence with childlike certainty.

Indeed, a cheerful confidence was a core characteristic of Joseph Ratzinger, the man; those who disagreed with him no doubt rejected such assuredness as unjustified. And yet, as he wrote in his fundamentally important book *Introduction to Christianity*, "Anyone who wishes today to make himself a spokesman of the Christian faith for people who are not rooted by profession or convention in the inner sphere of ecclesial speaking and thinking, will very quickly discover how alien and strange such an undertaking is." These words were written in 1968, the year of the student revolt and the encyclical *Humanae Vitae*. Since then, the situation of the church's proclamation in the prosperous countries has worsened. His later books have expressed this concern in urgent terms: for example, *Salt of the Earth*; and his last publication before becoming pope, *Values in a Time of Upheaval*.

An Intellectual Rooted in Faith

As Ratzinger turned seventy, he could still turn cold. There was not a trace of the proverbial Bavarian *Gemütlichkeit*, that easy, genial style that is said to be found in senior citizens. His exceptional learning and his wide theological reading were not always accompanied by personal warmth. His intellect sparkled, but one did not always see a human openness at the same time. And people wondered, politics aside, whether John Paul II could not have found a man more in harmony with his own personality for the position of prefect of the CDF.

To all appearances, though, Joseph Ratzinger lived in perfect harmony with the world of the Catholic Church. Perhaps he did not want to be disturbed in this world, or perhaps he saw his mission as communicating to Catholics this human equilibrium achieved on the basis of faith.

He also displayed in our conversations his qualities as an attentive listener, a theological master who was willing to hear arguments, analyses, and prophecies about the situation of the church decades after the close of the Council, and about the course it ought to be taking as the new millennium began. It sometimes happened that he accepted a better argument—but it had to be a *better* argument!

Because he possessed these qualities, the German cardinal was honored with membership in the Académie Française. On November 6, 1992, he was admitted as an "associate foreign member" in the section for "moral and political sciences." This was the first time that a German Catholic bishop was invited to join the most prestigious academy in the world, which Cardinal Richelieu, the prime minister of King Louis XIII of France, had founded in 1635. Ratzinger succeeded the then recently deceased Russian nuclear physicist and Nobel Peace Prize winner, Andrei Sakharov.

In the explanation for its bestowal of membership, the Academy spoke not only of Ratzinger's work within the church but also of his contribution as a scholar and bishop to the elucidation of questions of social morality and political theology. His razor-sharp analyses of social developments did not always meet with applause, and many thought that the medicine he recommended against the ills of our age was bitter. But he was often proved right later on. In his relationship to modern society, the cardinal seemed like a member of the 1968 generation, one whose late arrival on the scene allows him to make a correct analysis of the situation. Left-wing critique of society had taught Ratzinger that those who congratulate humanity for achieving prosperity are wildly premature.

This led him to show in a new way that the Christian message was relevant to our times. His views were more "left wing" than many of his "progressive" critics realized—and more "right wing" than was popular with the secular world of culture, which aims at assimilation and accommodation. The German cardinal in Rome, often misunderstood in his own country, found some consolation in the fact that the Académie Française paid tribute to the significance of what he had written on ethics and politics in a secular society.

When we celebrated his seventieth birthday, looking out far over Rome, the eternal city, he thought only briefly of these and many other honors, of all the honest eulogies and all the flatteries that had poured over him that day—and all those that he would still have to endure in the coming days. He reflected on all this with his skeptical, unfathomable gaze and with a great intellectual reserve. Then I said that all these honors were at any rate a confirmation of his own Catholic principle, namely, that it is only from a conviction which has been thoroughly examined that there emerges the power to create something new.

At that, he nodded.

The Prefect's Register of "Sins"

The list of Ratzinger's "sins" is long. During his period as chief guardian of Catholic orthodoxy, a great number of documents emerged from the CDF with his signature. These usually concluded with the statement that the pope had assented to their contents. Many in the church, however, dissented from these contents, and not a few saw them as an increasing scandal that was going on under the eyes of the pope.

Those who are interested in the details can look in the Internet at http://www.vatican.va/roman_curia/congregations/cfaith/doc_doc_index.htm, which offers a list of the statements with which Joseph Ratzinger will forever be associated in the minds of his critics. The following are some of the more memorable.

- Instruction on certain aspects of the "Theology of Liberation" (August 6, 1984)
- Notification on the book "Church: Charism and Power. Essay on militant ecclesiology," by Father Leonardo Boff OFM (March 11, 1985)
- Instruction on Christian freedom and liberation (March 22, 1986)
- Letter regarding the suspension of Charles Curran from the teaching of theology (July 25, 1986)
- Notification on the book "Pleidooi voor mensen in de Kerk" (1985) by Professor Edward Schillebeeckx, OP (September 15, 1986)
- Letter to the bishops of the Catholic Church on the pastoral care of homosexual persons (October 1, 1986)
- Instruction on respect for human life in its origin and on the dignity of procreation (*Donum vitae*, February 22, 1987)
- Formula to be used for the profession of faith and for the oath of fidelity to assume an office to be exercised in the name of the church (July 1, 1988)
- Instruction on the ecclesial vocation of the theologian (*Donum veritatis*, May 24, 1990)

- Note on the book *The Sexual Creators: An Ethical Proposal for Concerned Christians* (1986) by Fr. André Guindon, OMI (January 31, 1992)
- Instruction on some aspects of the use of social communications in promoting the doctrine of the faith (March 30, 1992)
- Letter to the bishops of the church on some aspects of the church understood as communion (May 28, 1992)
- Some considerations concerning the response to legislative proposals on nondiscrimination of homosexual persons (July 23, 1992)
- Formula to be used for the profession of faith and for the oath of fidelity to assume an office to be exercised in the name of the church, with the illustrative doctrinal note of the conclusive formula of "Professio fidei" (June 29, 1998)
- Considerations on "The Primacy of the Successor of Peter in the Mystery of the Church" (October 31, 1998)
- Notification regarding Sister Jeannine Gramick, SSND, and Fr. Robert Nugent, SDS (May 31, 1999)
- Documents regarding "The Message of Fatima" (June 26, 2000)
- Note on the expression "Sister Churches" (June 30, 2000)
- Declaration on the unicity and salvific universality of Jesus Christ and the church (*Dominus Iesus*, August 6, 2000)
- Doctrinal note on some questions regarding the participation of Catholics in political life (January 16, 2003)
- Considerations regarding proposals to give legal recognition to unions between homosexual persons (July 31, 2003)
- Letter to the bishops of the Catholic Church on the collaboration of men and women in the church and in the world (July 31, 2004)

This is not an exhaustive list of all the recent Vatican documents that have caused offense, since John Paul II himself published a number of "apostolic letters" that provoked severe criticism, especially in Germany and in the United States. Whether it was Ratzinger who prompted John Paul II or he who prompted Ratzinger, in the second half of the 1990s, the wave of outrage at Cardinal Ratzinger reached its peak.

A Deputy Pope for Germany?

In Germany, this criticism culminated in the conflict about church counseling services to pregnant women. According to state law, a woman who sought an abortion must first attend a counseling session, and this meant that any certificate attesting that she had been counseled—in whatever direction the counseling might have tended, including all counseling carried out through church agencies trying hard to work against the practice of abortion—could in fact be used to obtain an abortion. Many saw Cardinal Ratzinger as the spearhead of the opposition to this practice, but it should be borne in mind that the pontificate of John Paul II was characterized by a constant and vigorous rejection of abortion, both as an individual action and as a matter permitted by state legislation, especially in Western societies. The pope's aversion to abortion was completely certain, and he did not need Joseph Ratzinger or anyone else to prompt him to speak his mind on this topic.

The prefect himself was convinced on grounds of theological principle that the German practice was wrong; and when he took action on this issue, in a warning letter, personally approved by John Paul II, which was sent to the German bishops on May 20, 1998, he was only carrying out the will of the pope.

The response to this letter, as reported in the periodical *Herder Korrespondenz*, shows how difficult relations had become between German Catholics and Cardinal Ratzinger: "As a reaction to information in the press about Cardinal Ratzinger's letter of May 20, the Central Committee of the German Catholics [the highest lay body] has sent a letter to Bishop Lehmann (chairman of the bishops' conference) requesting him to intervene with the pope to stop the prefect of the Congregation for the Doctrine of the Faith from further attempts to exert pressure in the matter of counseling pregnant women in difficulties, and saying that if Cardinal Ratzinger genuinely wants the church to cease counseling pregnant women in difficulties, he will sabotage the united endeavors of the church in Germany to translate John Paul's concern about abortion into reality."

Bishop Lehmann of Mainz was thus supposed to open the pope's eyes to the alleged state of affairs: it was assumed that it was not he, John Paul II, who was spearheading the opposition to abortion and to the church's counseling practice in Germany, but Cardinal Ratzinger. And why was Ratzinger behaving thus? Highly placed persons in the German Catholic world, professors of theology, murmured that he wanted to "take revenge" for a whole list of slights. Even bishops agreed—naturally, all in a spirit of true Christian brotherhood. The Germans were asking John Paul II not to be more "papal" than his chief guardian of the faith. Was Joseph Ratzinger now a special commissioner of the pope for Germany? Or a kind of "deputy pope" for German-speaking Catholics?

As a result, the pope's September 1999 rejection of the Catholic certificate that made abortion possible without incur-

ring any legal penalties was felt as a crack of the whip, a humil-
iation of the bishops. Well-meaning Catholics saw it as a
catastrophe, and not a few suffered torments of conscience.
Others were infuriated and announced that they would no
longer be loyal to the pope. They appealed, as did Martin
Luther, to the true freedom of a Christian. But clearly, the pope
could live with the perception in Germany that he was a willing
tool of his own prefect.

Controversial Issues

This made the Bavarian cardinal's directory of "sins" longer
and longer. What about the discussion of the position of women
in the Catholic Church? For years now, there had been widespread demand for women's ordination to the ministry, so that
they could stand at the head of parishes as priests, as in other
denominations. In both Europe and the United States, where
many women study theology (usually with the intention of
becoming teachers of religion in schools) and where there are
many fully qualified women theologians, these demands were
often vociferous. In May 1994, John Paul II rejected these
wishes very clearly. This led several professors of theology in
Germany to assert that this question must be discussed on a
higher theological level than an apostolic letter by the pope—
with the result that the CDF made it clear that the pope's "no"
was a definitive church ruling.

Similarly, the "Instruction on Some Questions Concerning
the Collaboration of Laypersons in the Ministry of Priests"
(November 1997) seemed to have been drawn up with Germany
in mind. The sound financial situation there (thanks to the

state's church tax) and the valued tradition of the direct involvement of many committed Catholics in pastoral work meant that
there were more full-time lay church workers there than any-
where else in the world.

In this case, yet again, people saw the hand of Cardinal
Ratzinger at work, although the instruction was signed by eight
heads of Vatican congregations and pontifical councils, since it
touched on their specific areas of competence. The basic message of the instruction, which was written in the church's legal
language appropriate to its subject, was this: give to the layperson what belongs to the layperson, and to the priest what belongs
to the priest. But many, hoping for more flexibility, disliked the
boundaries drawn there between clergy and laity. Here too, it
was suspected that the German cardinal was on the warpath
against committed laypersons: he deprived them of their dignity,
it was thought, because he did not understand them.

Ratzinger's image was not improved when John Paul II promulgated a *Motu Proprio* "For the Defense of the Faith" at the
beginning of July 1998. This papal document listed guidelines
and obligations imposed by canon law on all who exercised the
ordained ministry or had been authorized by the Catholic
Church to study and teach theology. In order to make it perfectly clear that a particular obligation to fidelity was required
of professors and teachers of theology (even those who were
paid by the state), Cardinal Ratzinger did more than present the
papal document at a press conference; he also accompanied it
with a "Doctrinal Note." The requirement that professors
should make the profession of faith and take an oath of loyalty,
not only with respect to the state but also to the church, seemed
to have been made with Germany in mind, and many saw this as
a provocation.

The cardinal became a scapegoat once again when, at the end of June 1998, the hunt started for the "culprit" who was causing difficulties between the World Lutheran Federation and the Papal Council for Promoting Christian Unity with reference to the "Common Declaration on Justification." Only a few weeks earlier, Ratzinger told me personally that despite the good will to achieve a fundamental consensus, a number of points were blocking the path. If the Protestant side wished to emphasize not the endeavor to reach a consensus but the demand that everything had to be understood absolutely literally in the classical Protestant sense, then the Catholic Church could make the same demand on behalf of its own convictions.

Finally, at the beginning of September 2000, the Vatican issued the declaration *Dominus Iesus*, signed by Joseph Ratzinger and explicitly approved by John Paul II. Many took this as a signal that the Roman yoke must be definitively thrown off. John Paul II felt it necessary to say a few conciliatory words about the "separated brothers and sisters" in the other Christian churches and communities, but on the essential issue, he did not disagree with the prefect. The Catholic Church saw itself as the fullest and most complete expression of religious truth. While people outside the Catholic faith might come to salvation, the other religions of the world were, at best, quite deficient expressions of truth.

The Conversion of the Prefect

There was one key event during Cardinal Ratzinger's time at the CDF, and it happened very publicly for all the world to see. John Paul II had planned this for many years, and it was to involve his prefect.

The Catholic Church is the oldest great institution in the world, existing without interruption for two thousand years. On the threshold of its third millennium, it was to admit its errors of the past and make a confession of its sins in a solemn rite in Saint Peter's Basilica in Rome, asking humankind for pardon and begging God for mercy. The pope paid no heed to the doubts expressed by Cardinal Ratzinger and others in the church. He decided that the penitential service would be held on March 12, 2000, the Sunday following Ash Wednesday, as a sign of guilt and repentance.

In the service of the truth, the prefect of the former "Holy Office," the unassailable Inquisition, now had to admit guilt, after a candle had been lit before the crucifix. He did so with a poker face, but his heart was not unaffected by the words of the prayer he spoke:

> Let each of us realize that members of the church in the name of faith and morality, in their necessary commitment to protect the truth, have sometimes employed methods that do not accord with the gospel. Help us to imitate Jesus Christ, who is meek and humble of heart.

He might not have managed to say these words by himself, but John Paul II continued:

> Lord, you are the God of every person. In some periods of history, Christians have sometimes admitted the use of intolerant methods. By failing to follow the great commandment of love, they disfigured the face of the

church, your bride. Have mercy on your sinful children and accept our resolve to serve the truth in the gentleness of love, remaining conscious all the while that the truth can be enforced only with that power which belongs to the truth itself.

From the beginning of his pontificate in 1978, John Paul II had valued the obligation to tell the truth higher than the cautious calculations of the church politicians. He was not impressed by the objection that such an admission of sin might be seen by the church's critics as a definitive capitulation to the hostile tendencies of the spirit of the age. Nor was he swayed by the objections historians brought forward, that the leaders of today's church would be sitting in judgment in a cheap tribunal on the sinful Christians of yesterday. He remained unmoved in the face of the certain scorn the church's opponents would feel at a "spring cleaning" on the part of the papacy that was not accompanied by visible reforms. They would surely claim that there were still an awful lot of ecclesiastical sins left unconfessed. Joseph Ratzinger thought of all these points, too; perhaps they might have persuaded him not to take part in this rite. But he did so.

At this moment, Cardinal Ratzinger grew out beyond his vast knowledge, beyond the universe of his theology, and returned to the ordinary human world, so to speak. For naturally, he knew all the historical facts. Whenever he and I touched on a delicate topic in our conversations, he spoke with great openness and with historical accuracy, free of all partisanship. He was familiar with all the dark pages of the ancient and the more recent history of the Catholic Church, and he knew the guilt the papal church had incurred vis-à-vis the other Christian churches. He never wriggled out of uncomfortable historical questions concerning Spain or Latin America. He condemned anti-Semitism, no matter who had been guilty of it. He looked serenely at the past, and he was not afraid to open up the Vatican archives. He was fully convinced that the historical truth could only benefit the church, showing up the incorrectness of an anti-ecclesiastical or anticlerical reflection on the past. This, of course, meant the whole history, not some abbreviated version cut down to the size of a few headlines in the mass media.

He had written down a long list of sins, deviations from the spirit and teaching of the Christian gospel: the crusades and Inquisitions, with their use of intolerance and force against dissenters; the division of the one church of Christ and the wars of religion; contempt and enmity, as well as a hostile silence, in the church's relationship with the Jews; a failure to respect foreign peoples, cultures, and religions, sometimes linked to forced conversions; sins against the dignity of the individual and of humanity, against women, other races, and ethnic groups; sins against human rights and social justice. He never forgot all this.

From many of his remarks, it became clear to me that he could not simply engage in an intellectual discussion of the pros and cons. As prefect of the CDF, he had to make decisions, formulate judgments, and even issue condemnations. He had inherited the problem of the Jesuits, the most important priestly order in the church, when he assumed office, and he realized that if they did not pull themselves together, they would never regain their former greatness. He saw the theological weak points in Opus Dei, the influential lay organization founded in Spain; but he also valued their work on behalf of the church. He was afraid that liberation theology would lead to divisions among the clergy and to the introduction into church discourse of the ideology of the class struggle, which he regarded as a deadly poison. He would have been happy, other things being equal, to harness the zeal of a theologian like Leonardo Boff for a good Christian cause. The church could take a more relaxed attitude to military dictatorships based on power alone than to ideological regimes; and bearing in mind that not all the faithful were heroes, the church was often obliged to be very patient. Worldly power waned with the passage of time. It was much harder in the long term for the church to remain united in those countries traditionally reckoned as Catholic or Christian. The church was a mixture of heroes and cowards, saints and sinners. And of course, every critic was in possession of knowledge not available to those (like Ratzinger) who actually had to make the decisions!

He was impatient with stupid talk. If he was compelled to listen to it, he maintained an icy silence. He could behave with wounding arrogance when he talked to stupid people—or to clever politicians who wrapped up the pursuit of their own selfish interests in the mantle of Catholic good will. The prefect readily conceded that politicians had to seek reelection; but they should not put pressure on the church leadership to alter its principles, merely because they wanted another term in government. He knew that he was not making many friends among politicians when he said this. His first important mentor, Cardinal Frings, had the biblical motto: "Appointed to serve human beings." Joseph Ratzinger seemed always aware of still higher responsibility.

The prefect could react allergically when people seemed to want to turn the church into a self-service supermarket where they could "realize themselves" or obtain jobs for themselves. He evaluated the desire for women's ordination not simply in terms of dogma, but he asked what women could do better in (and with) the Catholic Church. In earlier ages, it was not "Rome" that supplied the answer to this question; it was courageous and selfless women, single or married, who invented the immense spectrum of Christian works of mercy—orders and congregations, missionary societies and social institutions, behind convent walls or in slums, in hospitals or schools, in stations for developmental aid, whether in the European Middle Ages or in today's Third World. Naturally, he knew that "not every woman can or should be like Mother Teresa." But it was women like her who gave society a Christian face, and indeed women were often the first to give society a human face. To reduce the Christian message to the slogans of feminism and summarize everything as a demand for women's ordination would be a failure to do justice to those tasks that are more urgently than ever required of Christians in our world—that was his view.

As pope, Benedict XVI would retain the elements in the coat of arms he had borne as archbishop of Munich and Freising, and then as cardinal in the Vatican, with its very "human" symbols— the Moor's head (symbol of the town of Freising), a bear carrying a burden on its back (an allusion to the legend of Saint Corbinian, the eighth-century French bishop who founded the church in Freising), and the shell, which recalls both pilgrimages and the legend of Saint Augustine. He has also retained his biblical motto *Cooperatores veritatis*, "fellow workers of the truth," since he is the vicar of Christ, of that Jesus of Nazareth who has never ceased to surprise people in all ages with his message of faith, hope, and love, of truth and of freedom.

Time of Transition

Four Cardinals at the Center

The world held its breath when Pope John Paul II died at 9:37 P.M., Saturday, April 2, 2005. Hundreds of thousands of the faithful from Rome and around the world came to Saint Peter's in Rome to pay their last respects to the deceased leader of the Catholic Church. They formed a gigantic queue: they cheerfully endured many hours of travel from great distances, and then a long wait—sometimes more than ten hours—in the Via della Conciliazione and Saint Peter's Square.

The cardinals, who now bore the responsibility for the church, bade farewell to the man who had been their leader and superior for over twenty-six years. It was he who had "created" them cardinals by giving them the red hat. But there was no time for the cardinals to engage in meditation. As the rules prescribed, they assembled for the first time on Monday, only two days after the pope's demise, for the first "general congregation."

It was neither personal ambition nor mere chance that determined whose voice was to be heard (literally and figuratively) in the Vatican on this occasion. A combination of centuries-old traditions and new regulations laid down by John Paul II himself in February, 1996, indicated who was to play a prominent role and make decisions during the *sede vacante*, in the period between the death of the old pope and the election of his successor, when the "chair of Peter" was vacant. In the next two weeks, four cardinals and two archbishops enjoyed a particular prominence. This did not determine in advance what would happen under a new pope; but it was important at the outset of the *sede vacante* and was to become even more important as time went on.

Canon law gave a prominent role to the *camerlengo*, the "Chamberlain of the Holy Roman Church," the Spanish cardinal Eduardo Martinez Somalo, born on March 31, 1927. A camerlengo upholds the rights of the Apostolic See after the death of the pope, because church law prescribes that as soon as the pontiff dies, all the offices to which he has made appointments in the Roman curia, the central administration of the church, automatically fall vacant. Those holding office must stop exercising the rights and duties of their various posts. From a secular viewpoint, the papacy can be considered an absolute monarchy; and in such a governmental arrangement this step is appropriate because it allows the new pope total freedom for his pontificate. It is only the camerlengo who makes the death of a pope official, and it is he who guarantees legal continuity in the Vatican.

This meant that the cardinal secretary of state, the Italian Angelo Sodano, born on November 23, 1927, was in fact no longer secretary of state. But as the former "prime minister" of the pope, he had far-reaching authority, supported in canon law by his position as subdean of the college of cardinals. This is why it fell to him to celebrate the first Requiem Mass for John Paul II on the day after his death and to offer the first evaluation of the deceased pontiff in his homily. The other cardinals recalled him—mostly positively—as a faithful executor of the papal will. As an experienced curial cardinal, he knew how to enforce the authority of the Vatican. But his Roman prudence made him reluctant to exaggerate the differences in a conflict. He was *papabile*, or at any rate a "grand elector," who would be able to gather votes for the candidate of his choice.

The dean of the college of cardinals was Joseph Ratzinger, born on April 16, 1927, who was now no longer prefect of the Congregation for the Doctrine of the Faith. He headed the body that would elect the new pope in the conclave. He did not indeed have the authority to lay down guidelines for the electors, but he could certainly give some pointers, and everyone expected him to do so. Cardinal Ratzinger never engaged in power politics. He never pursued political ambitions of his own, nor were there any protégés whose ambitions he supported. But one could be sure that he would step in, correcting errors or preventing developments where he felt that something or someone was not reliably Catholic. His unimpeachable correctness and his doctrinal authority were almost legendary among the cardinals. Anything that he approved during the *sede vacante* would certainly be above all suspicion; anyone whom he criticized would have little hope of becoming pope.

The vicar general of the pope for the diocese of Rome was the Italian Camillo Ruini, born on February 19, 1931. In practice, pastoral considerations meant that he retained his office after the pope's death, and so it was he who held the service of intercession in the pope's cathedral, the patriarchal basilica of Saint John Lateran, on the Friday before the pope died. Another source of influence was his presidency of the Italian bishops' conference, which gave him an unofficial precedence among the Italian cardinals. They were not as important and numerous as in the past, but they still formed the largest national group in the college.

The "minister of domestic affairs" and the "foreign minister" in the Vatican were the most influential among the archbishops. The Italo-Argentinian Leonardo Sandri, born on November 1943 in Buenos Aires, had been the "substitute" in the secretariat of state, responsible for matters within the church, and it was he who had read aloud the papal texts after John Paul II had lost the use of his voice. It was also he who told the news of the pope's death to the faithful in Saint Peter's Square, and hence to the world in general, on that Saturday evening. According to the regulations, it was he who now had to keep the administrative business of the Roman curia running.

The other "substitute" in the secretariat of state was the Italian archbishop Giovanni Lajolo, born on January 3, 1935 in Novara in Piedmont. Up to now, he had been responsible for relationships between the church and the countries of the world, and he retained this function in the transitional period. He would have to deal with the heads of state and of governments from all around the world who would attend the funeral of the pope. As apostolic nuncio in Berlin, he had shown that he was capable of shouldering heavy workloads.

Four cardinals stood in the limelight. And naturally, people wondered if one of them might be capable of even greater things. The cardinals themselves paid particular attention to one of their number, for it was Ratzinger who presided over their meetings. They observed that he did so "in an excellent manner."

But at once the objections came: a German could never become pope, for reasons of history and national psychology. Yet it was conceivable that Joseph Ratzinger, who would turn seventy-eight in a few days, on April 16, would breach this taboo. Whether he would in fact do so was a different question; the betting shops in London favored other candidates.

But the respected Milanese newspaper *Corriere della Sera* astonished most of its readers on Monday, April 4, by beginning the presentation of the *papabili*, the cardinals most likely to emerge as pope from the conclave in the Sistine Chapel, with the name of Joseph Ratzinger, who was portrayed under the headline:

Guardian of the faith, chosen by Wojtyla:
"Kindness consists in saying No."

One might have expected the "local man," Cardinal Dionigi Tettamanzi, the archbishop of Milan, to be mentioned first. But perhaps the journalists in Lombardy were thinking of the proverb: "One who enters the conclave as pope, comes out as a cardinal." When he opened the first general congregation after the death of John Paul II on the Monday morning, Ratzinger was aware that his colleagues were looking at him with particular interest, and he joked that this proverb was a consolation to him.

At such delicate moments, Cardinal Ratzinger put on his poker face—not exactly unfriendly, but not quite radiant, either—and one realized that he would have preferred to be doing research, investigating the basis on which theological affirmations and the church's political analyses were made. He was certainly not going to proffer any unconsidered remarks. And this was the persona he presented on the Monday in the Sala Bologna, a meeting room in the apostolic palace, when sixty-five men, their average age seventy years old, grown wise through their experience of life and of faith, took the first decisions about the *sede vacante*. Joseph Ratzinger presided, no longer as prefect—since that office was now vacant after the pope's death—but as dean of the college of cardinals. He spoke with the sober and focused authority of one who knew more than anyone else about most (indeed perhaps all) theological questions, and at any rate knew how to avoid mistakes.

Besides this, the German had already participated in two conclaves, in 1978, the year of three popes, when John Paul I and John Paul II were elected. He knew what was required now.

Stepping Out of the Shadow

The dean of the college of cardinals, Joseph Ratzinger, clearly knew what had to be done upon the death of the pope. This was laid down in the apostolic constitution *Universi Dominici Gregis*, promulgated by John Paul II in February, 1996, for the period of the *sede vacante* that would ensue upon his death. Only decisions on practical church matters were permitted during this time, not decisions on questions of greater importance, which might bind the hands of the new pope.

The most pressing task was to bid farewell to John Paul II. Even though in principle, the ancient rituals governing all the great ceremonies of the church remained valid, the ceremonies still needed to be well organized. Even more importantly, the cardinals—including those over eighty years of age, who were no longer permitted to vote in the conclave—had to discuss finding the right man to succeed him. The dilemma was obvious and inescapable: nothing and no one would have a stronger influence on the choice of the new pope than the man who had just died, John Paul II. On the preceding Sunday, Cardinal Angelo Sodano, hitherto his secretary of state, had called him *Magno*, "the Great"—a respectful title he clearly felt obliged to use. Whenever the cardinals met, whether in the official general congregations or in informal smaller circles, the figure of the dead pope was the decisive criterion in the search for a candidate. In these days, John Paul II was lying in state in Saint Peter's Basilica, venerated by the millions who filed past his bier.

The cardinals could not have behaved otherwise, even if they'd wanted to. Not only had almost all of them been created cardinals by John Paul II during his long pontificate (dean Ratzinger was one of the few exceptions), but also his person had made such a profound impression on them and on the church as a whole. His physical and intellectual impact, and the substance and the style of his period in office, were unforgettable. In a monarchical institution like the Catholic Church, the exceptional quality of John Paul "the Great" thus made the vacuum all the more painful. Hence, it was only now that the cardinals began to speak openly about individual colleagues, although they chose indirect and often veiled language: how would this or that brother "look" in the highest church office?— always compared to his predecessor. If an outsider walked up, they switched to talk of the lovely spring weather in Rome, complaining that the nights were cold. . . .

Even toward the close of the last pontificate, the cardinals disliked talking about his succession, not even as a preparation for the day that would surely come. The standard Latin formula about the pope during his lifetime calls him *feliciter regnans*, "happily reigning," and this always seemed to fit John Paul II. Certainly, it was never called into question by the princes of the church; he was an absolute monarch, and their respect for him had religious roots. This is why the "Most Reverend and Eminent Lords" (as the curial jargon calls them) seldom discussed the reigning pontiff among themselves, still less with outsiders, even in confidential conversations. One dimension of the "cardinal" virtue of prudence is the ability to hold one's tongue, even (or especially) when the reigning pope is gravely ill. If their conversation did turn to the subject of the pope, the cardinals expressed any criticism they might feel or any dissociation from papal actions by formulating prudent questions or adding a touch of clever irony. And observers suddenly realized that although the cardinals had a special relationship to the pope who had created them, they were not his "creatures" nor his slaves.

Only after the death of John Paul II were they able to speak openly and soberly about who should now succeed, and under what conditions. As far as possible, the person and the exercise of the papal ministry of his predecessor ought not be a burden for the new pope, but this could scarcely be avoided.

In the past, this has led to the rule of thumb, only half-joking, about the last few popes. From 1846 onward, a fat pope has been followed by a thin one; a pope with the letter "r" in his name has been followed by a pope without this letter. Giovanni Mastai-Ferretti (Pius IX, fat and "r") was followed by Gioacchino Pecci (Leo XIII, scrawny and no "r"); the next occupants of the chair of Peter were Giuseppe Sarto (Pius X), Giacomo della Chiesa (Benedict XV), Achille Ratti (Pius IX), Eugenio Pacelli (Pius XII), Angelo Roncalli (John XXIII), and Paul VI (Giovanni Battista Montini). Only Albino Luciani (John Paul I), a small, slight man, broke the sequence. Perhaps this was why he reigned only for thirty-three days and was replaced by Karol Wojtyla, a well-built man with the letter "r" in his name.

So now they had to look for a thin man!

Such jokes are born of the desire for change and continuity, both something new and something familiar. The successor ought to continue what his predecessor has done well, but his character and his public persona may well contribute something new. Or else he should improve what has been neglected and cut back what has been allowed to grow out of proportion. At the same time, he should resemble his predecessor in all that was exemplary.

A Tough Act to Follow

It was only now, in the preliminary discussions, that the church politics of the deceased pope were subjected to a detached and often ruthless analysis. Although the cardinals owed their elevation to the college precisely to the line taken by John Paul II, they were often swayed by more superficial, personal criteria. A pope may do his utmost to lay down the course to be taken by the bark of Peter, but few things are totally irreversible—and even small corrections of course can take a ship in a completely different direction.

After the lengthy pontificate of John Paul II, some held that young popes had disadvantages as time went by. A dynamic man like Karol Wojtyla, born in 1920, was elected pope in October 1978, after the sudden death of John Paul I, and he had given the church many fresh impulses. But his tempestuous style, always pressing vigorously forward, was not necessary for all popes. The cardinals recalled that John XXIII, elected at the advanced age of seventy-seven, had also provided many impulses in his short pontificate and that everyone had been sorry at his death, too. Even cardinals have a limited ability to plan what divine providence will ordain. After the longest pontificate in church history, the thirty-two years of Pius IX (1846–1878), from his fifty-fourth to his eighty-sixth year, they elected Leo XIII, who was then sixty-eight; and he lived to be ninety-three!

For the last five hundred years, it was always highly probable that one Italian would be succeeded by another. This sequence ended with the Pole Karol Wojtyla, but there seemed little likelihood that another Pole would be elected to succeed him. What about an Italian? One strong argument was always that they were electing a man to be bishop of Rome and primate of Italy: a promising candidate must have Roman or Italian experience, or at least speak the language of Dante, as Karol Wojtyla had done so charmingly on the balcony of Saint Peter's the night he was elected.

An argument in favor of electing a European was another papal title, "Patriarch of the West." The archbishop of Krakow had shown that there was no border between Western and Eastern Europe, and that the true boundary was with the non-Latin, Orthodox East. But, for that matter, nothing is impossible for God, and there is no need in the twenty-first century to engage in crusades to save the West. So why not elect an African?

This shifted the debate from allegedly external criteria such as nationality or skin color to geopolitical considerations. One European cardinal said that the difficulties experienced by the church in the West made a European pope necessary, but a Latin American cardinal countered that Europe had stood in the center of Christianity and the church for long enough. Two thousand years of puberty were over, and everyone had to grow up now: in short, the time had come to elect a man from the South. At the least such words could add an even greater sense of gravity to the discussion.

No matter how exceptional and exemplary the last pontificate had been, the cardinals began almost imperceptibly—and quite naturally—to note where wishes had remained unmet, or where wishes had arisen in the most recent past. The laudable firmness of John Paul II could now be seen as excessive rigidity, even as an old man's obstinacy. They were looking for someone who could also be a rock as far as the substance of doctrine was concerned, but who had a different style and made a different impact—a man who knew how to communicate with charm and friendliness, not someone like John Paul, who as Vatican insiders liked to put it used his naked fists to punch holes in any walls in front of him.

This analysis, however, did not always do justice to the past, for example, when the cardinals looked for a man who would be faithful to Catholic principles but would not drone on and on about them every day; or when it was observed that the new pope's face ought to display love toward people, not anxious concern; or when they sought a man who would not carry the burdens of the world on his shoulders, like Atlas, and who perhaps thought that everything depended on his own person, so that if he found it too difficult, everything would collapse into chaos. And then, a cardinal from the South remarked with a smile that they needed a pope who would hand back to God the responsibility for the world, and to Jesus, the founder of Christianity, the responsibility for the church. . . .

Some recalled John Paul I (1978) and John XXIII (1958–1963), both of whom were in sharp contrast to their predecessors. Both times, severity was followed by kindliness, a brooding personality by a man of serenity. But how could his successor add anything to John Paul "the Great" or present a contrast to him? The next pope ought to possess all the good qualities of John Paul—his indefatigable zeal as well as his high culture, his knowledge of the modern world and his religious piety, his active mobility and his contemplative silence, a heart for the poor and a grasp of global economic interconnections, his skill in communication through the mass media and his instinctive understanding of crowds. Up to April 2, it had been taken for granted that that was who a pope was. The successor of a great pope always finds it difficult; this time, it would be doubly so. The cardinals sighed, as they realized that it would not be easy to find the right one.

The Last Message of John Paul II

On Friday, April 8, six days after his death, John Paul II was buried in the crypt under Saint Peter's Basilica after the celebration of a solemn Requiem Mass in Saint Peter's Square. The Italian security officers estimated that about two million pilgrims and visitors from every corner of the world were present in Rome. Several hundred thousand pilgrims had come from Poland to honor their great deceased fellow countryman. In keeping with his office, the principal celebrant of the Mass was the dean of the college of cardinals, Joseph Ratzinger. Millions of Catholics and members of other religions in almost every country on the five continents followed the service on television and radio and were thus able to form an impression of the cardinal. The highest office-bearers of the Catholic church, cardinals and bishops in their red or violet vestments, more than two hundred heads of state and governments, representatives of international organizations, and leading representatives of the great world religions and religious communities bade farewell to the man who had led the Catholic Church for more than twenty-six years and had had a great influence on world politics.

After the readings from holy scripture it was Cardinal Ratzinger's task to give the homily. The dean of the cardinals presented the life of John Paul II as a continuing response to the one call "Follow me" received under changing circumstances— the passion for literature and for theater, confronting the terror during the invasion of Poland by Nazi Germany, the priestly ministry, the bishop among bishops.

Follow me! In October, 1978, Cardinal Wojtyla once again heard the voice of the Lord. Once more there took place that dialogue with Peter reported in the Gospel of this Mass: "Simon, son of John, do you love me? Feed my sheep!" To the Lord's question, "Karol, do you love me?," the archbishop of Krakow answered from the depths of his heart: "Lord, you know everything; you know that I love you." The love of Christ was the dominant force in the life of our beloved Holy Father. Anyone who ever saw him pray, who ever heard him preach, knows that. Thanks to his being profoundly rooted in Christ, he was able to bear a burden which transcends merely human abilities: that of being the shepherd of Christ's flock, his universal church. . . .

As Peter was the shepherd and suffered with Christ, said the homilist Ratzinger, so the aging and increasingly ailing John Paul II "has entered more and more into the community of suffering with Christ." He cited the deceased pope: "It is suffering that burns out evil through the flame of love and even bears from sin a diverse wealth of the good." Inspired by this vision, the pope had suffered and loved in communion with Christ; and therefore, the message of his life and death had been so clear and fruitful. And then, Ratzinger concluded:

71

All of us will forever remember how on that last Easter Sunday of his life, the Holy Father, marked by suffering, came once more to the window of the apostolic palace and one last time gave his blessing *urbi et orbi.* We can be sure that our beloved pope is standing today at the window of the Father's house, that he sees us and blesses us. Yes, bless us, Holy Father. We entrust your deal soul to the Mother of God, your Mother, who guided you each day and who will guide you now to the eternal glory of her Son, our Lord Jesus Christ. Amen.

After the Requiem, which lasted over two hours, the body of the pope was borne in a solemn procession into Saint Peter's and then to a simple vaulted funeral chamber in the crypt under the basilica. The earth received Karol Wojtyla: in accordance with the biblical admonition, dust returned to dust. After the Mass, in which millions had taken part, there was something almost disturbingly quiet about the burial of the mortal remains of John Paul II to the accompaniment only of venerable ancient chants and prayers. The church that had set the Pole from far-off Krakow at its head as priest and bishop, and which he had then led into the third millennium after its foundation by Jesus Christ, received him once again. Now, the only concern of the faithful was expressed in the prayers they had repeated beforehand in the solemn Requiem, that "his servant, whom God in his unfathomable design deigned to include in the ranks of the popes, might now in the heavenly kingdom receive eternal fellowship with him in whom he had hoped and believed." The same sentiment is expressed whenever the church prays for one who has died.

The great and the small of our world were present in Saint

Peter's Square in Rome at the burial of Karol Wojtyla, who had been the visible head on earth of the Catholic Church—and indeed, much more than just that—for a whole generation. The "great" of the church and of the world (who seemed small in the presence of this pope) took their places close up, to the left and right of the altar on which the dean celebrated the Requiem with its gestures and words steeped in meaning and sanctified by centuries of repeated use; the "small" (who had become great thanks to John Paul's defense of their dignity) were farther off, thronging Bernini's piazza with its colonnades, an innumerable multitude stretching along the Via della Conciliazione to the Castel Sant' Angelo, in the neighboring streets of the Borgo Pio down to the Tiber and across the bridges, as well as on many squares and in front of the Roman churches. In addition to the two or three million in the Eternal City, there were uncounted participants throughout all the earth. Never before have so many persons bid their respectful and sad farewell to one single man.

And that was truly how things were in those weeks in Rome: one man lay dying, and the whole world looked on, not out of curiosity, nor because the event was sensational, but because they were deeply moved by the way in which the pope was ending his life. After John Paul II was no longer able to speak, many stopped their pointless chatter about the meaning of life and death. And so, at the close of his long pontificate, voiceless and full of pain, he communicated one last message: the message of his own, utterly personal dying. In developed societies, where the individual's life expectancy is high, every progress in medicine in the last decades has intensified the fear with which people discuss the whole subject of "dying with dignity." The man Karol Wojtyla was now demonstrating what dying with dignity meant: his own death authenticated his testimony.

This was the final message of the pope on the day of his funeral, when he had no more words to speak, and all that was left was the rituals and prayers of the church. They spoke of trust in God; they spoke of another world. This may seem a matter of course, when the church buries a pope whom many regarded as the spokesman of all Christendom; but it was not some sense of official obligation that prompted John Paul II to display this courage in the face of death (which the old liturgy called a "return to the Father's house"). At the very end, in his pain, John Paul II could not conceal the uncertainty felt by the human creature as the physical powers decline and death draws near—but we also saw the strength of his Christian faith. Even those who did not share this faith could perceive its gentle presence. This faith is convinced of the Christian good news that death does not have the last word about the human person; that none of us is isolated in his own self; and that the human person is promised more than this earthly life. Now, the pope has "gone home" before the eyes of the world, opening for many people the doors to a forgotten and shuttered homeland.

With one simple image at the close of his homily, Cardinal Ratzinger beautifully expressed all this: *We can be sure that our beloved pope is standing today at the window of the Father's house, that he sees us and blesses us.* An unforgettable sentence.

Behind Closed Doors

Now the cardinals were on their own; they had buried the dead pope and did not yet have a living pope. But they became increasingly aware that they did have their dean, Joseph

Ratzinger, who presided over the general congregations with the same natural authority with which he had taken the chair at comparable meetings of the cardinals in the Vatican under John Paul II.

Now that the dignified funeral was past, the cardinals' concern was with the *status ecclesiae*, the situation of the Catholic Church in the world, and its future under a new pope. It was now their task to elect a new bishop of Rome "in due order, according to the prescriptions of John Paul II and the ancient rules," as the dean put it. And this in turn meant: "No interviews, and no private councils in the corridors!" The cardinals had in fact already begun doing precisely this. Many of them stopped in the streets to talk to a journalist or to give statements in front of a camera or a microphone. They excused themselves by saying that this was in the interest of the faithful, since the members of the church were now mature. And in any case, they were saying nothing of substance. The Vatican press spokesman, Joaquín Navarro-Valls, informed us that they would now stop talking to us. Besides this, the dean ruled that in the period before the conclave began, everything in the college of cardinals should be as transparent as possible: no wheeling and dealing in the backrooms.

Two of the cardinal electors, Jaime Sin (Manila, Philippines) and Adolfo Suárez Rivera (Monterrey, Mexico), were ill and asked to be excused from participating in the conclave. This left 115 cardinals who would enter the Sistine Chapel on Monday, April 18. The great theme in the background of all their discussions until then would be which of their number might be a good future pope; but any names mentioned in the media at that point were either the fruit of informed speculation or else simply plucked at random from the list of electors.

First of all, however, the senators of the church had to get the fullest picture possible of the situation in the church after the death of John Paul and of how things ought to go in the future. While nothing obliged them to subscribe to the gloomy assessment that the situation was particularly dramatic after the last pontificate and that the church faced the prospect of slow but certain extinction, there could be no doubt that some local churches in the West were facing extreme difficulties at present—in Western Europe, the United States, Canada, Australia, and New Zealand—that is, in the prosperous developed nations. The fact that the cardinals came from all parts of the world, however, meant that they had a more global vision, and their exchange of views helped relativize the negative findings.

The cardinals knew perfectly well that God and religion, Christianity and the church, propriety and morality had never had an easy lot at any period in human history. The message proclaimed by Jesus Christ was every bit as "inappropriate to the present age" and "incredible" two thousand years ago as it is today. When cardinals from Western countries lamented that the anchoring of the church in the people was disappearing fast, other cardinals comforted them by saying that such a church had never existed in *their* countries, and that the church did not in fact need this "popular" character. When a German or a North American reported worrying statistics of decline from his country, a cardinal from Latin America or India hid a smile, and then expressed his thanks for the financial support given by the rich dioceses to a building project in his own land.

The state of Catholicism in the northern hemisphere was well known throughout the world: the clamor for more democracy in the church, for a "slimmed down" sexual morality, for the abolition of celibacy, and for the ordination of women to the priesthood. It was often difficult for cardinals from other regions to understand this, still less to accept the positive elements in it. The frequent response: "Of course we must take the Western complaints seriously . . . but that cannot be the first point on the agenda. Let us begin by examining religious matters."

The cardinals of the Roman curia, such as Giovanni Battista Re of the Congregation for Bishops, demonstrated that the administration of the church was functioning normally and—bearing in mind that the church had over one billion members!—with relatively few problems. Clearly defined rules were of course necessary for the administration of a church with more than 4,200 bishops, with 2,600 patriarchal, metropolitan, archiepiscopal, and episcopal sees, 2,038 titular sees, numerous prelatures, territorial abbeys, exarchates and ordinariates, apostolic vicariates, prefectures, and administrative districts, with 110 bishops' conferences, and 19 regional synods. Wrong decisions had been made under John Paul II (due in part to the pope himself), but these would be inevitable in the future too; nor would the introduction of more "democratic" elements in the church prevent mistakes from happening. In order to replenish the ranks of the world episcopate, between 140 and 170 new bishops would have to be appointed each year. (The curial officials in the Vatican are not directly responsible for appointments below the episcopal level.)

Continuity or New Beginnings?

The cardinals from the great archdioceses throughout the world were well aware of a decline in numbers in many regions of the church, and particularly in the traditional pasture of

Christ's flock. Was this despite John Paul II, or rather because of him? An answer was not easy. The church's influence in society was diminishing, and many of the faithful had an increasingly loose relationship to the community of faith. New modern sects were competing with the church—and not without success. The numbers of priests and of men and women religious were sinking, sometimes rapidly. On the other hand, the fluctuations of church history display many ambiguous developments; decline in one region was perhaps compensated for by growth in another.

If one were to ask the men of the curia, the defenders of "Roman centralism," what this vast papal apparatus of secretariat of state, congregations and commissions, tribunals, councils and offices, committees, institutes, and institutions had to do with Jesus himself and what he stood for, one's criticism would receive the polite reply: It is precisely under the aegis of Rome that what Jesus stood for has become so huge and powerful. It is the job of the pope and the curia to consolidate the external ecclesiastical framework, which has to be the same throughout the world, so that every national church, whether in Canada or in Fiji, can develop its own life and each individual, whether in New York or in Berlin, can find the path to the blessed life with God through the endeavor to live his or her own personal faith.

We may note here that since the last conclave in 1978, the financial problems of the central offices in Rome had been solved. The Holy See had moved out of the red. Although John Paul II was not particularly interested in money, he saw to it that order was brought to the Vatican finances. This meant that it was not necessary to find a candidate versed in the world of economics—as had sometimes been the cardinals' priority at conclaves in the past.

Pragmatic electors, such as the United States' cardinals, asked in these days what guidelines should be followed in planning a new pontificate with a new pontiff. Has the world become more Catholic, more Christian, or more virtuous since 1978? Is the church booming or declining? Do Catholics feel better than they did twenty-five years ago? Ought one perhaps to *ask* them who they would like to see as pope? An ancient principle of church law stipulates that no one should be called to government "against the will of those involved." Another principle says: "What concerns everyone, should be decided by everyone." Ought one to hold a Gallup poll among the faithful? But might this not mean that the cardinal elected would merely be the man who had made the most beautiful promises, a man who declared his intention to change this or that point, or to retain this or that point in the church's life?

John Paul II had exercised his papal office with authority—there was no disagreement about that. He had not reduced the papal claims in the slightest, either within the church or in its external relationships; on the contrary, some cardinals objected that Rome's claims to authority had been extended beyond all reasonable proportions, and a very lively discussion erupted on this question. In the past, the front lines had been drawn between those zealous for the cause of religion and moderate cardinals more open to the world, or between progressives and conservatives. Now, the "papalists" and "conciliarists" of the Middle Ages had resurfaced in the party of the Roman centralists and the party supporting the local churches on the "periphery." In terms of church politics, it had perhaps not yet been realized how acute this division of views actually was; unless action was taken, it might harden into a definite polarization between the two groups. (It should, however, be mentioned here that the cardinals from the United States were genuinely grateful that they had received moral support from the pope in the pedophile scandals.)

This tension between the Roman center and the national churches is nothing new in church history. John Paul II had swept the stark division out of sight by means of his 104 trips throughout the whole world, as the chief actor in the church's mission and propaganda. We might say that the center was visiting the periphery. At the same time, of course, John Paul II intensified the same division, because now the pope and the curia were visible everywhere in the world. Many cardinals wanted a change of course here, although others thought that there was no need to act: things would get better on their own, they believed, especially if capable archbishops were appointed in the national churches. Besides that, not every pope would be so active and creative as John Paul, who had been a charismatic communicator of genius.

The Search for a Successor

When the cardinals emerged from the aula of the synod to the left of Saint Peter's after their deliberations, they said that they were not looking for a copy of the deceased pope. When they sat together in informal conversation in the evenings, they said that a "clone" of John Paul II was not what they needed. . . . In fact they were not supposed to be discussing individual personalities at all, but this was, of course, an impossibility!

Despite all the injunctions to observe silence, I did manage to hear various pieces of information. The search for a successor initially led the cardinals to consider Italian candidates—the archbishops of the most important dioceses in the country, Milan and Florence, but also the Italians who worked in the Roman curia. This was at the very least an act of politeness, after more than twenty-six years of a "foreign" pontificate in the heartland of the Catholic Church. But it also was a way of recognizing an important group of electors. Italy had the largest single contingent of cardinals, thirty-eight in all, twenty of whom were under eighty years of age and hence eligible to vote. (By comparison, there were eleven from the United States, and six from Spain and Germany.)

Attention then turned to Spanish- and Portuguese-speaking cardinals, not so much to the Europeans as to the archbishops from Latin America. One heard objections that the Latin Americans were divided among themselves and that the potential candidates had not published enough books to give proof of their theological qualifications. It was also pointed out that one could not make a man pope simply because it was opportune in geopolitical terms, or as a sign of good will, or because one wanted to recall to the world the importance of the poor. The only major counterobjection one heard to these arguments was that the Central Americans and Brazilians made up for any potential deficiencies by their considerable pastoral experience.

Then we heard that a large group of cardinals was becoming increasingly convinced that the German dean of the college was a candidate with good chances of success. There were, of course, from the outset cardinals had who called Joseph Ratzinger *papabile*, but now this possibility was beginning to emerge from the shadows of hypotheses and speculations; as mentioned earlier, the Italian newspaper *La Repubblica* reported on the Wednesday before the conclave that a considerable number of electors were now thinking along these lines, and all the information I myself had from Vatican contacts in the week before the conclave confirmed this. One heard that "between forty and sixty cardinals" were inclined to support Ratzinger; it was initially unclear whether this number referred to the entire college of 183 cardinals, to those who had taken part in the nine general congregations that had been held up to that date (ca. 140), or only to the 117 cardinals under eighty (two of whom were prevented by sickness from coming to Rome). It was also clear that some cardinals would not accept Ratzinger, not least because they feared that his reactionary reputation would provoke vocal opposition on the part of many groups in the church.

To the eyes of insiders, the Italian newspaper stories were even more telling than they appeared at first glance. The Italian newspapers have well-informed Vatican experts with good contacts to the Vatican, who write exclusively for the delectation of their readers about what goes on behind the walls of the world's smallest state. As important as what they were writing was what they were *not* writing—they were not writing about the prospects of the Italian candidates. By now, their favorite was the Bavarian cardinal. These reporters repeatedly pointed out that Ratzinger had been in Rome since 1982 and had won great respect in the eyes of cardinals and bishops from all the world. He was not only admired as a watchful guardian of Catholic doctrine, they added; more and more, his theology with its deep roots in the spiritual life came to be appreciated. Ratzinger had presented this theology in numerous books and articles, defending the faith and clarifying it in a way that attracted intellectuals.

Many "progressive" Catholics rejected the attitudes that he took so prominently; this was well known and did not escape the notice of his colleagues. He did, however, occasionally convince his critics, because his acute analyses of developments in modern society were usually accurate. At the same time, it was felt that most cardinals would not want a revolutionary in theology and church politics on the chair of Peter, but rather a "spiritual, reforming pope." After the general congregations and private gatherings that had taken place up to this point, this seemed to be the dominant opinion among the electors. Some even added that Cardinal Ratzinger had a more "open" position on some questions than the deceased pope.

Rising to the Challenge

Cardinal Ratzinger continued to exercise his office as dean of the college with a calm and natural manner. On that Wednesday, speaking in the huge audience hall to the diplomats accredited to the Holy See, he praised John Paul II's endeavors to promote peace. Since the reign of Paul VI, this audience hall has been the place where popes speak in public. Some remarked that Ratzinger "looked good there." This may have been a tad premature, but it was a widespread view—and only the conclave itself would reveal how widespread it actually was.

From that day, the tomb of John Paul II in the crypt below Saint Peter's was accessible to the public, and there came an increasing stream of visitors—tens of thousands, hundreds of thousands—above all, young people and Polish pilgrims.

Alongside the name of Joseph Ratzinger, the names of some Italian cardinals continued to be mentioned. But this group seemed unable to agree on one single *papabile*. The name most commonly heard was Tettamanzi of Milan, but others seemed to have objections to him. The Italian cardinals Re, Ruini, Scola, and Sodano were themselves "not impossible," one was told, but their real importance would be a weighty word spoken in favor of another candidate. The Italians appeared to want an Italian as their primate, after over twenty-six years of a Polish pontificate, but it was not likely that this patriotism would be strong enough on its own to overcome their differences in matters of theology and church politics. The longer they deliberated the less they could find common ground. I heard of this, despite the fact that Cardinal Ratzinger had reminded "his" cardinals once again of their obligation to keep silent in public. Well, I just decided not to let myself be counted as public! Thus, the preferences of the cardinals hardly remained hidden. It was said that a larger group of cardinals—"about sixty"—were openly supporting Ratzinger as their candidate. In the first votes, the required majority was 77 (of 115).

A smaller group favored the former archbishop of Milan, Cardinal Martini, not so much as a serious candidate of the reforming party—for Martini's health is too precarious—but as an alternative who might attract a growing majority. Carlo Maria Martini, seventy-eight years old, has preserved his dignified appearance in spite of his frailty and sickness; he now devotes himself to the study of the Bible in Jerusalem. Martini himself spoke in favor of his successor in Milan, Dionigi Tettamanzi, but reasons of church politics led the other Italians to withhold their support from him. The same is apparently true of four of the German cardinals (Kasper, Lehmann, Sterzinsky, and Wetter), who wanted to avoid handing victory on a platter to Ratzinger. They preferred to look for another candidate, while Meisner, archbishop of Cologne, was busy gathering votes for Ratzinger.

In the cardinals' deliberations, substantial questions about the future of the church received less attention: just as much time was taken up now by the examination of individual candidates. Almost all the cardinals with a chance of success—Joseph Ratzinger, now definitely the leading candidate, Italians from the great archdioceses or from the curia (Tettamanzi, Antonelli, Sodano, or Ruini), and pastors from Latin America—had now been mentioned, and the cardinals had evaluated their strong and weak points. This is why some cardinals, such as Martini and the chairman of the German bishops' conference, Lehmann, brought up substantial problems in the debate. One reason was their wish to remind the next pope that John Paul II had left some unfinished business.

It appears that the cardinals did not pay much attention to something many Catholics consider the main problem—the disproportionately centralized exercise of power by the pope through the Roman curia; linked to this are complaints about too little collegiality and democracy in the church. This may be because the cardinals, whether in Rome or in the dioceses, can themselves exercise direct influence and help correct these defects. As Cardinal Lehmann pointed out, the cardinals frequently encounter the need for a communications headquarters in the worldwide church—and that is how the Roman curia in fact sees itself.

During the meetings and discussions, the main problems were mentioned, well-known subjects that have been debated for years among Catholics, by bishops and by theologians, areas where it is felt that reforms are needed. One example is sexual morality and the guidelines issued by the church for marriage and family life. In this context, Cardinal Lehmann took up the problem of the admission of divorced and remarried Catholics to ecclesial fellowship and the reception of communion; many local churches experience this as an urgent matter. Another question is a "loosening up" of celibacy, the requirement that priests refrain from marrying; in the Latin rite, this is already possible in a few exceptional cases, and it has been normal practice for centuries in the Catholic Eastern churches. The cardinals also recognized the necessity of giving women greater possibilities than they've had in the past to work in the church, although they remained convinced that the ordination of women to the priesthood was excluded by the dogmatic pronouncements of the magisterium.

The cardinals began the conclave with a solemn Mass on Monday morning, April 18. This event was still open to the public. Once again, as the regulations prescribed, the principal celebrant in the liturgy at the high altar of Saint Peter's Basilica "for the election of a new pope who enjoys God's favor because of the holiness of his life" was the dean of the college, Joseph Ratzinger. All the cardinals attended, even those over eighty who would not eligible to vote in the conclave. Representatives of many countries and thousands of the faithful were present: the "people of God" were involved.

The high point of this service was the three readings from the Bible and the sermon by Cardinal Ratzinger after texts from chapter 61 of the prophet Isaiah, chapter 4 of the Letter to the Ephesians, and chapter 15 of the Gospel of John had been read. Just like a good rabbi in the synagogue or a Protestant pastor, Ratzinger knew the scriptures well and sought now to do nothing else than to expound on the sacred texts and show their relevance to our own day. The cardinals waited to hear what he would say. According to rumors over the weekend, many of them saw the German as *papabile*. I recalled

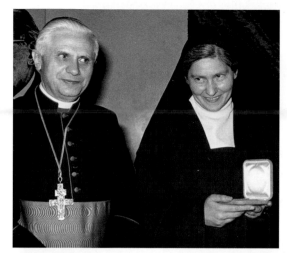

Cardinal Ratzinger presents the Romano Guardini Prize of the Catholic Academy in Bavaria, June 27, 1982, to the first woman to win this award, the Carmelite nun Gemma Hinricher.

Cardinal Ratzinger during the 2nd International Youth Meeting in Rome, March 30, 1985.

Cardinal Ratzinger during a discussion with members of the Working Party on the Catholic Press, November 26, 1984. (AKP)

Visit to Domaine la Bergerie near Annecy in Savoy, September 1988.

The Cross of Merit with Star of the Federal Republic of Germany is conferred on Cardinal Ratzinger by Chancellor Helmut Kohl in the residence of the German Ambassador to the Holy See, June 24, 1986.

Celebration of the 75th birthday of Cardinal Ratzinger in Rome, April 20, 2002: in conversation with his brother Georg.

Debate between Cardinal Ratzinger and Johann Baptist Metz, theology professor in Münster, Ahaus, October 27, 1998, on the occasion of Metz's 70th birthday.

Cardinal Ratzinger takes symbolic possession of the cathedral of Saint Aurea in the diocese of Ostia outside Rome, in a solemn Mass on March 16, 2003. The ancient diocese of Ostia is the traditional titular see of the dean of the college of cardinals. Ratzinger was elected dean of the six cardinal bishops in November 2002, and confirmed in this honorific office by John Paul II. (Photograph REUTERS/Max Rossi)

Cardinal Ratzinger and the renowned philosopher Jürgen Habermas met for a discussion in the Catholic Academy of Bavaria in Munich on January 19, 2004.

Pope John Paul II
and Cardinal
Ratzinger in Munich
during the pope's
visit to Germany,
November
15-19, 1980.

Pope John Paul II greets Cardinal Ratzinger in the audience hall in the Vatican,
February 6, 2004. (REUTERS/Pool)

Cardinal Ratzinger, Prefect of the Congregation for the Doctrine of the Faith.

Msgr Joseph Clemens from Siegen, a priest of the archdiocese of Paderborn and longtime secretary to Cardinal Ratzinger, on his appointment as bishop and Secretary to the Pontifical Council for the Laity.

The two German curial cardinals Joseph Ratzinger and Walter Kasper praise the "Family Catechism" (an explanation in epistolary form of the fundamental truths of the Catholic faith) by Winfried Henze, a priest of the Hildesheim diocese. He presented the cardinals with copies of his book in the palazzo of the Congregation for the Doctrine of the Faith on February 27, 2004.

Opening Mass of the conclave, April 18, in Saint Peter's.

Cardinals leaving the general congregation in the audience hall in the Vatican, April 15, 2005; Joseph Ratzinger in the foreground.

Archbishop Piero Marini closes the doors of the Sistine Chapel on April 18, 2005, after the cardinals gathered there for the conclave.

Black smoke was seen after the first round of voting on the evening of March 18, 2005.

that the old proverb was wrong: not everyone regarded as *papa-bile* did in fact leave the conclave as a cardinal. In the conclaves of 1939 and 1963, Eugenio Pacelli and Giovanni Battista Montini were the favorites, and they were elected as Pius XII and Paul VI.

I had seldom seen cardinals listening so attentively as during the sermon of their dean at the high altar of Saint Peter's, where usually only the pope—for the last twenty-six years, of course, that had been John Paul II—celebrates Mass. Now it was a seventy-eight-year-old German who stood there in their midst, and the tension in their faces showed that they were analyzing his words with great care.

No one knew the cardinals—those in the curia and those in the great archdioceses of the world—better than Joseph Ratzinger. He had headed the CDF for decades, and he had spoken innumerable times at consistories and synods. Not a few cardinals had taken offense at his unambiguous choice of words, and some had been outraged at the harshness of his verdicts. But not even his fiercest critics could dispute the clarity of his intellect; even when they disagreed, there was a nagging doubt that perhaps his analyses might be offering the right recipe for the church's leaders, although they were a bitter medicine, prescribed by a strict master.

The dean had presided with great skill over the general congregations after the death of John Paul II. Even when he insisted that they observe silence in their dealings with the media, this had been welcomed as a liberation from tiresome questions; only a few of the more loquacious cardinals had seen it as a muzzling. Now, all were asking themselves whether one could imagine this German as pope.

Was it a nod to Protestant Christians that the first reading from Isaiah asserted the Protestant principle "Because God is a rock eternally." God and not foremost Peter is the rock—that was the message. The present leaders of other Christian churches will have heard this. Significant also was Ratzinger's interpretation of the second reading from the letter of the apostle Paul to the Ephesians. The text reads:

> until we all attain to the unity of the faith and of the knowledge of the Son of God, to mature humankind, to the measure of the stature of the fullness of Christ; so that we may no longer be children, tossed to and fro and carried about with every wind of doctrine, by the cunning of men, by their craftiness in deceitful wiles.

Inevitably, Cardinal Ratzinger found that the apostle's words, written down two thousand years ago, "concern us directly at this time." His view of the intellectual, cultural, and ecclesiastical situation seemed to many listeners like the program for a future pontificate:

> How many winds of doctrine we have known in recent decades, how many ideological currents, how many ways of thinking. . . . The small boat of thought of many Christians has often been tossed about by these waves—thrown from one extreme to the other: from Marxism to liberalism, even to libertinism; from collectivism to radical individualism; from atheism to a vaguely religious mysticism; from agnosticism to syncretism, and so forth. Every day new sects are created and what Saint Paul says about human trickery comes true, with cunning which tries to draw others into

error. Having a clear faith, based on the creed of the Church, is often labeled today as a fundamentalism. Whereas relativism, which is letting oneself be tossed and "carried about with every wind of doctrine," looks like the only attitude acceptable to today's standards. We are moving toward a dictatorship of relativism, which does not recognize anything as certain and which has as its highest goal one's own ego and one's own desires.

Cardinal Ratzinger's response to this attitude is the teaching of the Catholic Church: "We have a different goal: the Son of God, true man." The dean said that Christians must be loyal to this truth:

> Being an "adult" means having a faith that does not follow the waves of today's fashions or the latest novelties. A faith that is deeply rooted in friendship with Christ is adult and mature. It is this friendship which opens us up to all that is good and gives us the knowledge to judge true from false, and deceit from truth. We must become mature in this adult faith; we must guide the flock of Christ to this faith.

A Cardinal's Manifesto

Those cardinals who were well versed in theology knew at once that Joseph Ratzinger had not simply made up this list of ideologies and modern, fashionable intellectual currents. One can read them in the documents of the nineteenth- and twentieth-century popes—for example in Pius IX, who reigned from 1848 to 1878 in the longest pontificate of church history and gave Christendom not only the dogmas of the Immaculate Conception of Mary (1854) and papal infallibility (1870) but also a "summary of errors." He did so shortly after becoming pope in 1846, when he was still regarded as a "liberal," in his encyclical *Qui pluribus*, and he did it again in 1864 in the encyclical *Quanta cura* and the *Syllabus errorum*. In the same way, Pius X (1903–1914) employed decrees and oaths in his fight against the errors of the Modernists. In September 1907, his encyclical *Pascendi dominici gregis* was a strikingly powerful onslaught on Modernism. Its opening words, "the flock of the Lord must be cared for," take up words used by Jesus in the Bible when he speaks to Peter, the prince of the apostles and first bishop of Rome. The same words are found in the constitution with which John Paul II regulated the *sede vacante* period and the election of the pope in the conclave. And they echo in the closing words of Joseph Ratzinger's homily on April 18, 2005: "We pray with insistence to the Lord, so that after the great gift of Pope John Paul II, he again gives us a pastor according to his own heart, a pastor who guides us to knowledge in Christ, to his love and to true joy. Amen."

Now the cardinals had to make up their minds. Under Pius X, Pius XI, and Pius XII, everything smacking of "progress" had been discredited in the minds of many Catholics (and indeed of most other Christians at that time). Many people still felt that being "Catholic" meant a slavish obedience to the Roman magisterium, renouncing one's own powers of thought. The reforms introduced under those three popes did not harm the general upward trend in church life; on the contrary, the church had never experienced such a flourishing at any time in its history until the Second Vatican Council was convened in 1962, with the young Joseph Ratzinger as one of the theological experts. In its four sessions, the Council opened up the church and entered a hopeful dialogue with the very "errors and mistakes of the age" that it had once lamented.

Other cardinals were posing a different question at lunch that Monday. What if "Ratzinger's manifesto" is in fact not reproducing accurately the commission of Jesus Christ to Peter, "Feed my sheep"? What if it would, in fact, be more true to say that the leaders of the church, its cardinals and bishops, are on a pilgrimage throughout the course of time together with the "people of God"? They do not possess more knowledge than the laity, because Christianity is convinced that truth lies in God. And the laity, who are all very good and well intentioned, do not really need to be "led." And if they do need a leader, then he ought to be mild! And was not Ratzinger talking about problems of European intellectual history, which seem anachronistic in a church that today is spread around the globe, problems that are no longer central?

The dean's sermon did not make the election easier. But it made the issues at stake clearer.

The Conclave Begins

A solemn procession of 115 cardinals electors made its way on the afternoon of April 18 from the Hall of Benedictions in Saint Peter's Basilica to the Sistine Chapel. It is here that the conclaves have been held since the late Middle Ages, with some interruptions, and they have taken place here in an unbroken sequence since 1878. The electors are totally cut off from the outside world: the word "conclave" comes from the Latin *cum clavi*, emphasizing that they are locked in "with a key." Before proceeding in a secret election to choose the successor of Pope John Paul II, the cardinals prayed for divine assistance, which they surely needed in view of the difficult task of leading with absolute papal authority such an immense community of faith scattered throughout the world, in the footsteps of a man many were already calling "the Great." (Many Polish Catholics, indeed, want him proclaimed the patron saint of Poland.)

The regulations envisaged two votes in the morning and two in the afternoon, beginning with a first vote on Monday evening. Smoke signals from a chimney on the roof of the Sistine Chapel indicate the outcome of the votes: black smoke means an unsuccessful vote, but white smoke leads to the official proclamation, *Habemus papam*, "We have a pope!" The man elected needed seventy-seven votes, two-thirds of the electoral college plus one.

Once again, this procession of the highest dignitaries of the church demonstrated that the person at the center of the dynamic was still Pope John Paul II. For a whole generation, during the stormy pontificate of John Paul II, the cardinals had always stood in his shadow, and this was inevitable in simple optical terms: the one figure in white was clearly distinct from the other figures in red. Just ten days ago, it was Karol Wojtyla, as he lay in death, who attracted everyone's gaze. More than a few cardinals now felt orphaned.

This feeling was justifiable, for the cardinals of the Holy Roman Church are "created" by the pope: it is he alone who decides on membership in the highest body in the leadership of the Catholic Church. Since virtually all the cardinal electors in 2005 had been created by John Paul II—one of the two exceptions was Joseph Ratzinger—it was natural that they should feel as if they had lost a father. However, this need not dictate the future. Not all sons are repetitions of their fathers.

One last time, however, the main person was missing in this measured procession, with its dignified pomp and the chants of the litany of the saints. We would not see so many cardinals again until the cardinal protodeacon proclaimed: We have a pope again. *Habemus papam.*

Thanks to the absence of the two sick cardinals from Asia and Latin America, the Europeans had once again—presumably for the last time—an absolute majority over all the other continents taken together (fifty-eight to fifty-seven). Naturally, the cardinals themselves were perfectly well aware that the absolute majority of the world's Catholics lived in North and South America. These were very different regions; the North American cardinals, especially the eleven from the United States, tried to have good relations with their brethren from the South, but they felt some unease about their pious exuberance, especially on social and political questions.

The Europeans may have been the majority, but they had always held a diversity of views. Joseph Ratzinger and Carlo Maria Martini believed the same faith, but they differed on how this faith should be put into practice in the life of the faithful and the church as a whole. And Karl Lehmann of Mainz crossed national boundaries when he attempted to gather votes for the Italian.

Fourteen cardinals came from North America, twenty-one from Latin America, eleven from Africa, eleven from Asia, and two from Oceania.

The twenty Italians were the largest national group, and it would perhaps have been natural for them to have the largest number of *papabili*. But, as we saw, they had not reached any consensus in the period before the conclave. This recalled the conclaves in 1978, when the two favorites, Siri of Genoa and Benelli of Florence, had sufficient votes to block each other, so that an alternative candidate was elected, first Albino Luciani in August, then Karol Wojtyla in October. Might history repeat itself in 2005?

The eleven electors from the United States had taken hard knocks in the pedophile scandals, which had exceedingly unpleasant consequences for their image and their finances. They had no ambition to present a candidate of their own and were no more united as a group than the six Germans, the six Spaniards, the five Frenchmen, or the three Poles. The four other national groups of any size, the four Brazilians, four Mexicans, three Columbians, and three Canadians, could not agree on whether reforms would help the church, and if so, which reforms and how extensive these ought to be. Nor did they agree on a candidate who could square the circle, bringing about changes in an institution in which venerable old traditions played an essential role. Should one retain that which was tried and tested, or try out something unfamiliar? Their average age, somewhat over seventy, could work both ways, encouraging either caution or experimentation. Perhaps the wise old men might see that some traditions had become rigid and ineffective; or perhaps they might see that one must hold on patiently to the tradition in the flux of fashions.

At any rate, we may say that the cardinal electors needed the cardinal virtues—prudence, righteousness, courage, and moderation—for the conclave. This was emphasized by the

Czech Jesuit Cardinal Tomas Špidlik, who delivered a sermon in the Sistine Chapel in which he offered a meditation on papal elections. The cardinal virtues derive their name, like the "cardinals" themselves, from the Latin word *cardo*, "hinge," the point on which everything turns. In the first millennium, the Roman church under its bishop had twenty-four important churches, then at a later period several districts under the leadership of a deacon, and seven "suburbicarian" dioceses. Those who held these responsibilities gradually became the most important collaborators, helpers, and counselors of the bishop of Rome, and they came to share in his ecclesiastical authority, which itself was gradually extending beyond the eternal city, northward over the Alps.

In the first millennium, the pope was elected democratically by the people, although this election was too often preempted by the warring aristocratic families, who simply appointed a pope. The German kings intervened to stabilize the exercise of the highest spiritual office in the West, and this meant that the Roman cardinals became the sole electors of the pope. Pope Nicholas II, formerly Gerhard of Burgundy (1059–1061), saw in the college of cardinals the structural instrument that canon law offered to cope with the crisis that occurred every time a pope died; this permitted him to extricate the highest church ministry from secular power struggles and conflicts of interest, so that the papacy would no longer be dependent on kings, noble dynasties, or the people itself. It would be freed from simony and lay investiture.

Nicholas II, in his zeal for church reforms, also wanted to put an end to the purchase of ecclesiastical offices, to make a clearer distinction between the laity and the clergy, and to prevent the secular world from encroaching on the sphere of the church. He wanted to avoid any irregularities or doubts about the legitimacy of an election; interventions by outside persons were also to be precluded. Quite a list! In 1059, a synod of bishops laid down definite rules for the papal election, and these were confirmed by the papal bull *In nomine Domini*, the earliest decree on this subject. This envisaged a mutual process of renewal: the cardinals would elect the pope, who would create new cardinals, who in turn would elect the pope. . . .

One later factor was the extension of the college beyond Rome. From the end of the twelfth century on, bishops from outside Rome were made cardinals, thus constituting a kind of world senate of a church that embraced all the peoples. Initially, there were thirty cardinals. Sixtus V laid down in 1586 that they might not number more than seventy. John XXIII abolished this limit, and today there are 183 cardinals, no more than 120 of whom may be electors of the new pope. After Cardinal Špidlik's meditation, the double doors of the Sistine Chapel were closed, and at least in human terms, the cardinals were completely on their own.

A Spiritually Fruitful Election

The master of ceremonies, the Italian archbishop Marini, cried: *Extra omnes!* All had to leave the Sistine Chapel, and the cardinals were alone on Monday afternoon, April 18. And yet they were not completely alone: here too, John Paul II was present, with the dramatic words from no. 83 in his constitution governing the conclave:

> And finally, I exhort the cardinal electors with the same insistence as my predecessors that they are not to let

themselves be guided in electing a pope by sympathy or antipathy. They are not to be influenced by favors shown, nor by their personal relationship to a person, nor are they to allow their choice to be determined by the interference of high-standing persons or pressure groups, nor by the influence of the means of social communication, by violence, fear, or the desire for popularity. Rather, they are to keep their eyes fixed only on the honor of God and the well being of the church. After invoking divine assistance, they are to give their vote to that person (even if he is not a member of the college of cardinals) whom they judge to be most suited to govern the universal church in a manner that brings blessings and benefits to all.

The senators of the church may also have sensed that they dare not disappoint the expectations of millions of believers. They may have recalled what the deceased pope had prescribed, in order to give them spiritual strength:

During the *sede vacante* period, and especially during the time in which the successor of Peter is being elected, the church is united in a very special way with its pastors, and especially with the cardinals who are electing the pope. The church beseeches God for a new pope, who will be the gift of the divine goodness and providence. That is why the entire church must follow the example of the earliest Christian community mentioned in the Acts of the Apostles, who were spiritually unanimous in prayer together with Mary, the mother of Jesus. This will mean that the election of the new pope is not an event isolated from the people of God, something that would concern only the electoral college. In a sense, this election will be an act of the whole church. I decree therefore that, after the news of the vacancy of the Apostolic See is made known, and especially after the death and the burial of the pope, humble and persistent prayers be raised to the Lord in all cities and towns, or at least in the most important of these, asking that he may enlighten the cardinal electors and lead them in the performance of their task to such a unity that there may be a quick, harmonious, and spiritually fruitful election, as is required for the salvation of souls and the good of the entire people of God.

"That there may be a quick, harmonious, and spiritually fruitful election!" This could not happen in the first vote, nor did it need to do so. Smoke arose from the chimney of the Sistine Chapel, on which the eyes of the whole world were turned, after the first vote on Monday evening, and after the second and third votes on Tuesday morning. Against the gray Roman skies, it always seemed gray, never unambiguous. The onlookers could be sure that the smoke was black only because the bells of the basilica, set to ring when the new pope had been chosen, remained silent.

And then it happened.

Accepted in Humility

It was on the fourth vote. Joseph Ratzinger's prayers were of no avail. He admitted, a few days later, that he had begged

God to spare him "this guillotine." The majority in favor of his candidacy grew. Indiscretions suggest that he received far more than the necessary two-thirds majority plus one (seventy-seven). Some cardinals say that he received more than one hundred votes—a genuine plebiscite. And perhaps the cardinal dean then took to heart these other words of John Paul II in no. 86 of the constitution:

> I ask the one who is elected not to flee from the office to which he is called because he is afraid of the burden it entails, but to accept in humility the plan of the divine will. For it is God who imposes the burden on him, and it is God who will also support him with his divine hand, so that he is able to bear it. The one who gives him a difficult task also gives him the aid needed to fulfill it. When he bestows the dignity on him, he also gives him the strength not to be crushed under the burden of this office.

After a conscientious counting of the votes in the inner chapel under Michelangelo's "Last Judgment," the outcome of the fourth vote was announced. Once again, the constitution came into force—it was, after all, not exactly the same kind of election as that of a national president—and several cardinals noted that the canon lawyers had foreseen even this case, namely, the election of the dean of the college. An ancient ritual now began (nos. 87 and 88):

> Once the election has been carried out according to canon law, the last of the cardinal deacons calls the secretary of the college of cardinals and the papal master

of ceremonies into the electoral chamber. Then the cardinal dean or [!] the highest ranking and oldest cardinal, in the name of the entire electoral college, asks the one elected whether he accepts election: *Do you accept your canonical election to the papacy?* As soon as he has received the assent, he asks him: *What name do you choose?* The papal master of ceremonies, who acts as notary, and has as his witnesses two assistant masters of ceremonies (who are summoned to the place of election at this point), draws up a document recording that the new pope has accepted his election and his choice of name. As soon as he accepts election, and provided that he has already received episcopal ordination, he is bishop of Rome, true pope and head of the college of bishops; he receives at once full and supreme authority over the universal church and can exercise this without delay.

A few hours later, four of the German cardinals—Lehmann, Meisner, Sterzinsky, and Wetter (some of whom were bubbling over with happiness, although their moods did vary somewhat)—sat in the German priests' college to the left of Saint Peter's, the Campo Santo Teutonico, alongside the huge audience hall, and told journalists that there was a great collective sigh of relief as soon as Cardinal Ratzinger accepted his election. He went to put on his new garments, which had been rather unfittingly made by the papal court tailor Gammarelli— the white cassock was far too short—and then he presented himself to the cardinals. Joachim Meisner, cardinal archbishop of Cologne, is seldom at a loss for words, even strong words, but he was struck dumb and could only weep. Benedict XVI knew what he had to say to him: "I will come to the World Youth Day in Cologne." Then they embraced.

This part of the proceedings is described by the constitution in sober language:

> After the customary formalities prescribed by the *Order of the Rituals of the Conclave* have been carried out in the meantime, the cardinal electors come forward in the prescribed manner to pay their homage to the newly elected pope and to promise him obedience. This is followed by a prayer of thanksgiving in common, and then. . . .

And then . . . the excitement was palpable in Saint Peter's Square around 5:40 that Tuesday evening. It seemed that something was about to happen, and that was strange. For people had reasoned that if the first vote in the afternoon was inconclusive, there was no need to communicate this by means of a smoke signal—the cardinals could have waited until seven o'clock that evening, after the second vote. And then . . . the crowd, more and more numerous, murmured that the first smoke was rising. It was impossible to be sure of the color. (The cardinals subsequently admitted that they had difficulties with the oven: the smoke had penetrated the Sistine Chapel, where they were sitting, instead of going out through the chimney.) And then . . . there came more smoke, not unambiguously white, but certainly not unambiguously black. And then . . . the bells began to ring.

And then . . . the constitution prescribes:

> The first cardinal deacon proclaims to the waiting people that the election has taken place, and the name

of the new pope, who immediately after this imparts the apostolic blessing *Urbi et Orbi* from the loggia of the Vatican basilica.

Smoke had risen from the chimney at 5:40, although its color was not clear. At 6:04, the bells began to ring—first the heavy bell high up in the bell tower on the façade of the basilica, then the small bells too. And then . . . the bells of all the Roman churches joined in, together with countless bells throughout the world. The news of a successful election spread like the wind through the Eternal City, and Romans and visitors ran to Saint Peter's Square. Many millions now followed the events on television.

Pope Benedict XVI

In the Vineyard of the Lord

First, the protodeacon of the cardinals, the Chilean Jorge Arturo Medina Estévez, stepped out on the center loggia of Saint Peter's and spoke the expected words first in Spanish, then in other languages, and finally in Latin: "*Habemus papam.*" But right after the "*Josephum,*" with unmoved facial expression he made an artificial pause. Then the name Ratzinger was already drowned in the cheers of the 100,000 people in Saint Peter's Square. His name: Benedict XVI. A sensation.

The newly elected pope himself came out, Benedict XVI, Joseph Ratzinger.

He seemed relaxed after the strenuousness of the last weeks. He waved and greeted the enthusiastic crowd on the Piazza with both arms, yet still reserved—as if by no means did he want to exaggerate. His appearances seemed less spectacular than that of his predecessor. But his joy and the warmth of his heart could not be missed.

He said only a few words to the crowd that had swelled to more than 100,000 of the believing and the curious.

DEAR BROTHERS AND SISTERS, after the great pope, John Paul II, the cardinals have elected me, a simple and humble worker in the Lord's vineyard.

The fact that the Lord can work and act even with insufficient means consoles me, and above all I entrust myself to your prayers.

In the joy of the resurrected Lord, we go on with his help. He is going to help us and Mary will be on our side. Thank you.

With few gestures, Benedict XVI had introduced himself into his new ministry; with an economy of expression, he began displaying his new style.

The Pope from Bavaria

Everything argued against Joseph Ratzinger as the new pope. A German from Bavaria, dean of the college of cardinals, a representative of Roman centralism, the prefect of the Catholic invigilation office, an inexorable Grand Inquisitor, in whose eyes the bloodless purity of the faith was more important than human beings, an arrogant Catholic whose outlook was preconciliar and unconciliatory, a man who refused to enter into dialogue with other Christian churches and non-Christian religions, a theological reactionary, insensitive to the signs of the times. For many years now, all these accusations had been leveled at him. He lacked modernity—or so we were told, time and time again.

But the cardinals, the only people who counted in the context of a conclave, obviously took a different view. They knew of no one better suited to succeed the great John Paul II than the seventy-eight-year-old Joseph Ratzinger from Marktl am Inn. In the course of twenty-four hours, at least two-thirds of the electoral college had become certain he was the right man; those who for whatever reason had hesitated, doubted, or pursued other goals were now in the minority. And such a large majority in favor of Ratzinger surely had their reasons.

Proud of Being Catholic

Joseph Ratzinger, now Benedict XVI, enters upon the difficult inheritance of the papacy, which is evaluated so very differently by Christians, adherents of the world's religions, and "people of good will." This is not only the inheritance of his immediate predecessor but that of all the other bishops of Rome and successors of the apostle Peter. From the perspective of the last papacy, which lasted almost an entire generation, it is as if the new pope's task would be to set the final coping stone in the vault, holding everything securely in place. With tireless activism, as the leading and the best propagandist of his immense flock, John Paul II began to build in many areas where the work must be continued; he also left behind a number of problems, which must be resolved by means of well-considered reforms. The very fact of choosing the name *Benedict* revealed "to the city and to the world" that the new pope intended to go behind the Johns and Pauls and Piuses of recent decades to take up the tradition of the past and continue it in the future. *Andiamo avanti!*, the new pope cried, "Let us go forward!" He certainly intends this slogan to be taken seriously.

In this election, the cardinals from all the world—both from prosperous societies and from the poor countries of the southern hemisphere—have told their new head, the new pontiff of the church, that they pay no heed to prejudices. They are not afraid to choose "a German" (in many parts of the world, the word still has a negative connotation). They trust his wide Christian training, his encyclopedic theological erudition, his gift for eloquent expression in many languages, his sense of moderation, and his clear delight in life. The new pope also benefits from the cardinals' experience of the long pontificate of John Paul II: the Petrine ministry is no longer just an infallible central office, inspiring fear in people. International mediation is carried out in Rome, where cardinals and archbishops under the pope's guidance seek to achieve mutual understanding among the national churches, without ever forgetting the responsibility they bear to the community of peoples.

Pride in being Catholic was another factor in Joseph Ratzinger's election. He was seen as a guarantee of Catholic substance, and he will make good on his promise. In some countries, other Christians appear to believe that Catholics belong to the church only against their will and that their real wish is for the church to keep on changing so that vigorous transformations will "modernize" the religious world with which they are familiar. Once again, the cardinals took a different view. If Benedict XVI is to fulfill their expectations, the faithful must ask, not only what the new pope can do for them, but also what they themselves can do for the community of Jesus of Nazareth, whom the new pope calls our "friend."

Blessings That Flow from a Name

During a walk Cardinal Ratzinger took in the last days before the conclave, he spoke about his favorite papal name: *Benedict* sounds good. The Italian *Benedetto* sounds even better;

and so many wonderful melodies for the Mass have been composed to the Latin form *Benedictus*. And then there is Saint Benedict, the father of Western monasticism fifteen hundred years ago. One can also interpret the name theologically: the man elected by the cardinals in conclave after the invocation of the Holy Spirit must be "blessed," the answer to their prayer, otherwise there would be no point in his accepting the election. The last pope with this name, Benedict XV, was elected at the outbreak of the First World War and died in January 1922. Another point in its favor would be the change of name after all the Johns and Pauls and Piuses of the nineteenth and twentieth century. Yes, he would like the next pope to have the name Benedict XVI.

But he was not talking about himself. Not about what name *he* would choose! The dean of the college of cardinals had never envisaged himself as a successor to the great pope from Poland, and he had never done anything to promote himself as a candidate. He was the loyal theological assistant to John Paul II, and that was all. He had more than enough to do to keep healthy, with the enormous burden of work in his twenty-three years as prefect of the Congregation for the Doctrine of the Faith; and he wanted to be able to continue studying theology and deepening his knowledge of the "science of the faith" in his few free hours. As the author of numerous books, he was not without his own ambitions: he was happy when others found spiritual and intellectual profit from reading his work. He hoped to consecrate the last years of his life entirely to his beloved theology, once he was relieved of his curial office at the age of seventy-five (which he had asked John Paul II to allow, following canon law). Initially, he had thought of studying contentedly in his native Regensburg, but more and more he had come to appreciate

Rome as the place to spend his retirement, since the Eternal City played so great a role in Christian theological culture.

All these dreams came to nothing, nor will they ever come to anything. John Paul II was unwilling and indeed unable to do without his theologian cardinal, and Joseph Ratzinger could not turn down the pope's request to continue in office, given that the pope too did not abdicate—even when a purely rational calculation might have indicated that the demands of the papal office far exceeded his strength. The cardinal revered the Holy Father and regarded him as a friend, although he sometimes found himself forced to shrug his shoulders and accept the pope's activism, John Paul's tremendous urge to express himself—a quality foreign to Ratzinger. All this made it impossible for him to think of resigning his office at the head of his Congregation in the Vatican.

The older Joseph Ratzinger became, and the more John Paul II declined into physical frailty, the stronger was the authority of the cardinal, who was both resolute and personally modest. So strong was his position that a large group of cardinals knew the name of John Paul's successor as soon as they began to meet after the death and burial of the pope: it had to be Joseph Ratzinger, not on the basis of personal politics but as a quite spontaneous certainty. They believed that their dean was capable of exercising the highest office in the Catholic Church. Even before the conclave had started, people were talking of forty, fifty, or even sixty electors who would choose Ratzinger, and this huge number, not far short of the votes necessary to attain the prescribed two-thirds majority (77 votes out of 115 electors), developed its own momentum and came to influence the minority ever more strongly. Those who hesitated, for whatever reason, had now to ask themselves why they should *not* elect the German dean, in view of the fact that so many of their colleagues wanted him as pope.

Cardinal Ratzinger did not pay attention to any such speculations when we spoke together: he simply liked the name *Benedict*, not for himself but for someone else. Certainly, he was intelligent enough to realize that it was possible that he too might ascend the throne of Peter, but to begin with, he dismissed the idea. Since Hadrian VI (1522–1523), Hadrian Florensz from Utrecht, no German had been elected pope. And although Utrecht was in the Holy Roman Empire at that time, the Dutch did not take kindly to the idea that Hadrian was German! To find a "real" German, one would have to go much further back, to the eleventh century. Controversial events in the twentieth century had made a German pope completely impossible, although it was in fact a pope, Pius XII, who elevated Germans (Frings, Preysing, and von Galen) to the cardinalate in 1946 as a deliberate consolation to the German people after the Second World War.

As the cardinals researched the matter, they wondered: The Pole Karol Wojtyla, John Paul II, was born in 1920 in Wadowice, a Polish town not far from Auschwitz, the most horrible concentration camp in the history of the genocide of the Jews. Joseph Ratzinger was born in 1927 in Marktl am Inn, not far from Passau, the bishop's see, but much closer to the Austrian town of Braunau, where one of the greatest criminals in human history, the most evil seducer of the German people, was born in 1889. It would only be the "merit" of a "late birth" that took Ratzinger out of direct involvement with this history, and the fact that during his childhood in an orthodox Catholic family, as a teenage helper of an anti-aircraft unit and as a prisoner of an American camp, he experienced only the negative sides of the

Nazi regime. "A lot of distress for an unmilitary person as I am," he writes in his memoirs.

Grateful Devotion to the Church

When Joseph Ratzinger spoke to me about the Catholic world in Bavaria in which he grew up, as someone raised in the Berlin diaspora, I felt how wonderful it must have been. In the world outside, the dictator Hitler ruled and there was war, then an oppressive postwar period, and yet it seemed to have been a happy life for the schoolboy and the student of theology. It is obvious that he has never found "Catholicism" to mean prohibitions against doing things one would have liked to do or frustration at narrow rules and the lack of necessary reforms. I do not believe that the "beauty" of the Catholic faith is something that Ratzinger is just imagining, projecting it back onto his early years. It is in fact the basis on which his whole life is built, and a gift that others did not receive. It has given him a wholly natural devotedness to the church, which his critics probably cannot genuinely feel. For the cardinals, this is the brilliant background against which some of his doctrinaire harshness has to be judged. Thanks to his early years, Joseph Ratzinger is a "positive" man. It is not because of some intellectual laziness that he "dismisses" criticism of the church; rather, he sees more strongly the small and happy beauties of life. In theological terms, he has already said this in the few words with which he presented himself on Tuesday evening on the central loggia of Saint Peter's: what counts is the "joy," the "glory of the risen Lord Jesus Christ." It will now be his task as pope to teach this to others, to get this Christian message across in modern society.

The cardinals knew almost all the details of Joseph Ratzinger's ecclesiastical career, beginning with his priestly ordination on June 29, 1951. They knew that even as a young theologian, he was not looking for the structural changes that are incessantly demanded in the church; he wanted inner forms, vitalized by the spirit of faith. He was not impressed when Catholics—bishops and theologians and committed laypersons—wanted to invent the church anew, dynamically and fundamentally, and yet were unable to do so. When they were conducting the choir, the musically gifted Ratzinger refused to sing. He simply kept silent when harsh critics or self-aware young women told him how he ought to be governing the church. His strong point (at any rate up to now) has not been an easy conversational style, cheerful pastoral work among the people, hectic organization, or the strategies of power politics. The curial cardinals appreciate this, because they know that Benedict XVI will not interfere in their offices and their areas of competence. The crowd on Saint Peter's Square on Tuesday evening already noted his reserve and perhaps sensed that something was missing—Benedict XVI is not a populist! But it is possible that the cardinals not only accepted these "deficits" in comparison to John Paul II as something they just had to put up with. It is in fact possible that they deliberately sought such qualities. After a turbulent pontificate, more calm was needed in the central administration of the church.

And yet, their choice was surprising. The fact that he was prefect of the CDF and dean of the college argued against his election. It had not been customary in the past to give the Grand Inquisitor of the church and the highest ranking cardinal the fullness of papal authority. The dean is often regarded as the epitome of curial rigidity and of the Roman centralism that does all it can to block the collegiality sought by the bishops of the universal church. Well, it seems that the cardinals did not object too strongly to all the doctrinal clarifications and the disciplinary measures that issued from his office in all these years. Those who actually took the trouble to read the decrees of the Congregation properly were often surprised by the sheer amount of progressive ideas in these texts—they left to others the business of protesting. The dry documents often contained prophetic words, as in the case of the clarification on liberation theology, issued in 1984, which, as we saw, called communism the "shame of our times." And those who wished to be completely fair to the Grand Inquisitor of the church read the books and articles that Joseph Ratzinger produced "on the side." How he managed to be so productive is a little miracle in itself.

Sermon of a Lifetime

Pope Benedict XVI delivered an address in Latin to the cardinals in the Sistine Chapel barely twelve hours after his election. An outsider listening to the address might have wondered how Joseph Ratzinger had entered the conclave with the full text of an inaugural speech in his pocket. But in fact it was an example of his extraordinary intellectual productivity , and it did not surprise me. I had experienced him in situations of intellectual creativity, when he had a thousand things to do and appointments to keep, yet worked with precision, hardly ever making a mistake. Joseph Ratzinger knew what he wanted to say to the cardinals as pope, and he knew how to formulate his ideas.

This allowed him at his first address on that Wednesday after his election to indicate at once a number of guiding principles for his pontificate. As he spoke concentrating on his words, he seemed relaxed. Because Benedict XVI spoke in Latin not all of the cardinals understood everything. All the more focused though, they studied the translation into several world languages. They were sure that this speech had to be remembered.

GRACE AND PEACE IN ABUNDANCE TO ALL OF YOU!
(see 1 Peter 1,2)

In my soul there are two contrasting sentiments in these hours. On the one hand, a sense of inadequacy and human turmoil for the responsibility entrusted to me yesterday as the successor of the apostle Peter in this See of Rome, with regard to the universal church. On the other hand, I sense within me profound gratitude to God, who—as the liturgy makes us sing—does not abandon his flock but leads it throughout time under the guidance of those whom he has chosen as vicars of his son, and made pastors.

Dear Ones, this intimate recognition for a gift of divine mercy prevails in my heart in spite of everything. I consider this a grace obtained for me by my venerated predecessor, John Paul II. It seems I can feel his strong hand squeezing mine; I seem to see his smiling eyes and listen to his words, addressed to me especially at this moment: "Do not be afraid!"

The death of the Holy Father John Paul II and the days that followed were for the church and for the entire world an extraordinary time of grace. The great pain of his death and the void that it left in all of us were tempered by the action of the Risen Christ, which showed itself during long days in the choral wave of faith, love, and spiritual solidarity, culminating in his solemn funeral.

We can say it: the funeral of John Paul II was a truly extraordinary experience in which was perceived in some way the power of God, who, through his church, wishes to form a great family of all peoples, through the unifying force of Truth and Love. In the hour of death, conformed to his Master and Lord, John Paul II crowned his long and fruitful pontificate, confirming the Christian people in faith, gathering them around him and making the entire human family feel more united.

How can one not feel sustained by this witness? How can one not feel the encouragement that comes from this event of grace?

Surprising every prevision I had, Divine Providence, through the will of the venerable cardinal fathers, called me to succeed this great pope. I have been thinking in these hours about what happened in the region of Caesarea two thousand years ago: I seem to hear the words of Peter: "You are Christ, the Son of the living God," and the solemn affirmation of the Lord: "You are Peter, and on this rock I will build my church. . . . I will give you the keys of the kingdom of heaven."

You are Christ! You are Peter! It seems I am reliving this very Gospel scene; I, the successor of Peter, repeat with trepidation the anxious words of the fisherman from Galilee, and I listen again with intimate emotion to the reassuring promise of the divine Master. If the weight of the responsibility that now lies on my poor shoulders is enormous, the divine power on which I can count is surely immeasurable: "You are Peter, and on this rock I will build my church." Electing me as the bishop of Rome, the Lord wanted me as his vicar, he wished me to be the "rock" upon which everyone may rest with confidence. I ask him to make up for the poverty of my strength that I may be a courageous and faithful pastor of his flock, always docile to the inspirations of his Spirit.

I undertake this special ministry, the Petrine ministry at the service of the universal church, with humble abandon to the hands of the Providence of God. And it is to Christ in the first place that I renew my total and trustworthy adhesion: *In Te, Domine, speravi; non confundar in aeternum!*

To you, Lord Cardinals, with a grateful soul for the trust shown me, I ask you to sustain me with prayer and with constant, active, and wise collaboration. I also ask my brothers in the episcopacy to be close to me in prayer and counsel so that I may truly be the *servus servorum Dei* (servant of the servants of God). As Peter and the other apostles were, through the will of the Lord, one apostolic college, in the same way the successor of Peter and the bishops, successors of the apostles—and the Council forcefully repeated this—must be closely united among themselves. This collegial communion, even in the diversity of roles and functions of the supreme pontiff and the bishops, is at the service of the church and the unity of faith, from which depend in a notable measure the effectiveness of the evangelizing action of the contemporary world. Thus, this path, upon which my venerated predecessors went forward, I too intend to follow, concerned solely with proclaiming to the world the living presence of Christ.

Before my eyes is, in particular, the witness of Pope John Paul II. He leaves us a church that is more courageous, freer, younger. A church that, according to his teaching and example, looks with serenity to the past and is not afraid of the future. With the Great Jubilee the church was introduced into the new millennium carrying in her hands the gospel, applied to the world through the authoritative rereading of Vatican Council II. Pope John Paul II justly indicated the Council as a "compass" with which to orient ourselves in the vast ocean of the third millennium. Also in his spiritual testament he noted: "I am convinced that for a very long time the new generations will draw upon the riches that this council of the twentieth century gave us."

I, too, as I start in the service that is proper to the successor of Peter, wish to affirm with force my decided will to pursue the commitment to enact Vatican Council II, in the wake of my predecessors and in faithful continuity with the millennia-old tradition of the church. Precisely this year is the fortieth anniversary of the conclusion of this conciliar assembly (December 8, 1965). With the passing of time, the conciliar documents have not lost their timeliness; their teachings have shown themselves to be especially pertinent to the new exigencies of the church and the present globalized society.

In a very significant way, my pontificate starts as the church is living the special year dedicated to the Eucharist. How can I not see in this providential co-incidence an element that must mark the ministry to which I have been called? The Eucharist, the heart of Christian life and the source of the evangelizing mission of the church, cannot but be the permanent center and the source of the Petrine service entrusted to me.

The Eucharist makes the Risen Christ constantly present, Christ who continues to give himself to us, calling us to participate in the banquet of his body and his blood. From this full communion with him comes every other element of the life of the church, in the first place the communion among the faithful, the commitment to proclaim and give witness to the gospel, the ardor of charity toward all, especially toward the poor and the smallest.

In this year, therefore, the solemnity of Corpus Christi must be celebrated in a particularly special way. The Eucharist will be at the center, in August, of World Youth Day in Cologne, and, in October, of the ordinary Assembly of the Synod of Bishops, which will take place on the theme "The Eucharist: Source and Summit of the Life and Mission of the Church." I ask everyone to intensify in coming months love and devotion to the Eucharistic Jesus and to express in a courageous and clear way the real presence of the Lord, above all through the solemnity and the correctness of the cele-brations.

I ask this in a special way of priests, about whom I am thinking in this moment with great affection. The priestly ministry was born in the Cenacle, together with the Eucharist, as my venerated predecessor John Paul II underlined so many times. "The priestly life must have in a special way a 'Eucharistic form,'" he wrote in his last letter for Holy Thursday. The devout daily celebration of Holy Mass, the center of the life and mission of every priest, contributes to this end.

Nourished and sustained by the Eucharist, Catholics cannot but feel stimulated to tend toward that full unity for which Christ hoped in the Cenacle. Peter's successor knows that he must take on this supreme desire of the Divine Master in a particularly special way. To him, indeed, has been entrusted the duty of strengthening his brethren.

Thus, in full awareness and at the beginning of his ministry in the Church of Rome that Peter bathed with his blood, the current successor assumes as his primary commitment that of working tirelessly toward the reconstitution of the full and visible unity of all Christ's followers. This is his ambition; this is his compelling duty. He is aware that to do so expressions of good feelings are not enough. Concrete gestures are required to penetrate souls and move consciences, encouraging everyone to that interior conversion that is the basis for all progress on the road of ecumenism.

Theological dialogue is necessary. A profound examination of the historical reasons behind past choices is also indispensable. But even more urgent is that "purification of memory" that was so often evoked by John Paul II, and which alone can dispose souls to welcome the full truth of Christ. It is before him, supreme judge of all living things, that each of us must stand, in the awareness that one day we must explain to him what we did and what we did not do for the great good that is the full and visible unity of all his disciples.

The current successor of Peter feels himself to be personally implicated in this question and is disposed to do all in his power to promote the fundamental cause of ecumenism. In the wake of his predecessors, he is fully determined to cultivate any initiative that may seem appropriate to promote contact and agreement with representatives from the various churches and ecclesial communities. Indeed, on this occasion too, he sends them his most cordial greetings in Christ, the one Lord of all.

In this moment, I go back in my memory to the unforgettable experience we all underwent with the death and the funeral of the lamented John Paul II. Around his mortal remains, lying on the bare earth, leaders of nations gathered, with people from all social classes and especially the young, in an unforgettable embrace of affection and admiration. The entire world looked to him with trust. To many it seemed as if that intense participation, amplified to the confines of the planet by the social communications media, was like a choral request for help addressed to the pope by modern humanity, which, wracked by fear and uncertainty, questions itself about the future.

The church today must revive within herself an awareness of the task to present the world again with the voice of the One who said: "I am the light of the world; he who follows me will not walk in darkness but will have the light of life." In undertaking his ministry, the new pope knows that his task is to bring the light of Christ to shine before the men and women of today: not his own light but that of Christ.

With this awareness, I address myself to everyone, even to those who follow other religions or who are simply seeking an answer to the fundamental questions of life and have not yet found it. I address everyone with simplicity and affection, to assure them that the church wants to continue to build an open and sincere dialogue with them, in a search for the true good of humankind and of society.

From God I invoke unity and peace for the human family and declare the willingness of all Catholics to cooperate for true social development, one that respects the dignity of all human beings.

I will make every effort and dedicate myself to pursuing the promising dialogue that my predecessors began with various civilizations, because it is mutual understanding that gives rise to conditions for a better future for everyone.

I am particularly thinking of young people. To them, the privileged interlocutors of John Paul II, I send an affectionate embrace in the hope, God willing, of meeting them at Cologne on the occasion of the next World Youth Day. With you, dear young people, I will continue to maintain a dialogue, listening to your expectations in an attempt to help you meet ever more profoundly the living, ever young, Christ.

"Mane nobiscum, Domine!" Stay with us, Lord! This invocation, which forms the dominant theme of John Paul II's Apostolic Letter for the Year of the Eucharist, is the prayer that comes spontaneously from my heart as I turn to begin the ministry to which Christ has called me. Like Peter, I too renew to him my unconditional promise of faithfulness. He alone I intend to serve as I dedicate myself totally to the service of his church.

In support of this promise, I invoke the maternal intercession of Mary Most Holy, in whose hands I place the present and the future of my person and of the church. May the holy apostles Peter and Paul, and all the saints, also intercede.

With these sentiments I impart to you venerated brother cardinals, to those participating in this ritual, and to all those following us by television and radio, a special and affectionate blessing.

After the Mass, the Pope was happy to share lunch with the cardinals in the Vatican Santa Marta guesthouse, where all of them had lived throughout the conclave period. He also went quite simply and naturally for a walk, visiting his former office at the Congregation of the Doctrine of the Faith, where he talked with his former colleagues. He also then passed by his former apartment outside the Vatican, to the joy of the Romans.

"I Am Very Deeply Moved"

The Romans were delighted to see the new pope be nice, kiss babies, meet people with genuine human warmth, and let them get close to him. Yes, they had worried a little about the German. Because, really, the pope is their bishop—well, admittedly, he is also the bishop of the world. . . . But first, as the Romans see it, first come the Romans; the pope has been foremost their bishop for the last two thousand years, and they need a bishop who can show a few emotions, too. They want to feel good when they think of him and speak to their children of the "Papa," when they hold up a baby to him for a kiss. And so they were very happy to see Benedict XVI emerge from the Vatican on Wednesday evening, exactly twenty-four hours after his election by the cardinals. He left his new home to visit his old apartment in the Piazza della Città Leonina. He was obliged to travel most of the way in a limousine, although it was only a short trip and he would have preferred to go on foot. But finally he was able to get out of his car and walk in the crowd in his white papal robes. He uttered the decisive words: *Sono emozionatissimo,* "I am very deeply moved!" These words turned the German into a Roman.

Joseph Ratzinger had lived in Rome since the end of 1981 and had usually gone on foot from the square outside the Vatican walls, across Saint Peter's Square, to his office in the palazzo of the Congregation for the Doctrine of the Faith, to the left of the colonnades. He wore a black cassock; in the colder months, he wore a black beret over his snowy hair. He carried a black briefcase, somewhat battered by years of use. Things could continue like that, said the Romans—but now he would have to wear white!

Late in the evening of the day after the election, I took one of Joseph Ratzinger's books down from my shelves, one of the many that I had acquired in the years of our friendship, in the years when we were both in Rome. I have two copies of this book on my "Ratzinger shelf." First, there is the seventh edition of the first version, which I bought long ago out of curiosity to see what kind of "Introduction to Christianity" a theologian was writing in 1967/1968, those turbulent years, to explain the significance of the faith to young people. What a tremendous amount of criticism of Christianity, the church, and religion there was at that time—though of course, there is always a lot of criticism, and perhaps that is why Joseph Ratzinger, as professor, archbishop, cardinal, dean, and now pope, reacts with serenity to criticism. He once wisely observed that one does not always take criticism with full seriousness, since the one who bears responsibility must take decisions in his own sphere—and the critic seldom realizes how little he or she actually knows about that sphere.

I experienced something similar myself, as "our man in Rome" with the duty of reporting for a great daily newspaper about events, declarations, and decisions in the Vatican. This included the job of reporting about those who visited Cardinal Ratzinger in his office or had other dealings with him. I would have made things much easier for myself if I had joined in the mighty chorus of "anti-Roman" voices and become a zealous conformist, contributing my own strokes of the paintbrush to the picture of the "reactionary in the Vatican who knows nothing of the real world." I believe it was a much greater intellectual adventure to attempt to understand for myself what was going on in the central administration of the Catholic Church.

This act of understanding was certainly not invariably positive and uncritical; but I trust that I myself and my readers grasped that the oldest large-scale organization of world history is not condemned to disappear in the immediate future. It will accompany humanity and individual human beings for some time to come. As a political correspondent, I also wrote about Italian society and politics and about the Italians themselves.

Sometimes, the anger readers felt—their indignation, their personal hurt, or their puzzlement—at decisions taken by Cardinal Ratzinger or requests he had refused, or at decrees and "doctrinal notes" of his congregation, was directed to the messenger, not just to the message, for the simple reason that my account was not couched in tones of vigorous rejection. Since my aim was to promote understanding, I deliberately wrote in a neutral style, irrespective of what my own personal feelings on the well-known thorny topics might be. As my predecessor as correspondent of the *Frankfurter Allgemeine Zeitung* in Rome once remarked, a journalist does not need consolation in times like that; all he needs is "skin as thick as an elephant's." And I was happy to learn that Cardinal Ratzinger too read my "products." He told me once that he was reading my theological novel *The Laughter of the She-Wolf* each evening, from start to finish, although it was 650 pages long. I cannot imagine a greater compliment.

"My Yoke Is Easy, My Burden Is Light"

My books by Ratzinger also included a completely revised edition of the *Introduction to Christianity* with a new foreword, published in 2000. I started to read, and came upon formulations I found daring: "Religion has become 'modern' again." I turned the pages and came across the "Upanishads, Confucianism, and Taoism," or phrases such as "the fear of Christian 'imperialism'" and "homesickness for the lovely plurality of the religions and their supposedly original serenity and freedom," which gave a taste both of other world religions and of the astonishing erudition of the author. One question stuck in my mind when the author, then prefect of the CDF, commented on the lords of the modern global future: "Does this not mean that a new ruling class will take into its hands the keys of existence, the administration of the human person?" The church faced a conflict with other powers who wanted to gain control of public opinion and rule over souls. Joseph Ratzinger always gave me food for thought.

That was true now, just as it had been true about forty years earlier when Joseph Ratzinger, at the time professor at the University of Tübingen, could not get out of his head one of the fables of the Brothers Grimm, "Johnny in Luck" (a fable he also writes about in his original foreword to the *Introduction to Christianity*).

We might employ worldly categories and say that perhaps this book put his feet on the first rungs of Ratzinger's "luck," that is, his career in the church, because an Italian translation landed on the writing desk of Paul VI, pope at the time, who was an unhappy man after the rejection of *Humanae vitae* (1968), his encyclical on the transmission of human life. Paul VI had little "luck" with his Catholics, so many of whom refused to obey him on the questions of contraception and birth control, and many non-Catholics and concerned non-Christians reacted to his encyclical with incomprehension and even outrage. But that is another story—though one with which Joseph Ratzinger, now Pope Benedict XVI, will have to come to grips.

"Johnny in Luck" is the story of a servant who serves his master for seven years and is paid with a piece of gold "as big as Johnny's head." But as he is carrying it home, it becomes too heavy for him, and he barters it for other things to make his burden easier: he exchanges the gold for a horse, the horse for a cow, the cow for a goose, the goose for a grindstone—and then the grindstone falls into a well. The fable concludes: "With a light heart and free from every burden, he then sprang away until he was at home with his mother." It almost sounds like one of God's "flower children," but this can scarcely have been the pedagogical meaning of the fable. Surely all it is saying is that Johnny was too foolish for his own good?

Joseph Ratzinger certainly understood the last sentence of the fable in a profoundly ironic sense—*Johnny Unlucky*, as it were. Johnny has thrown away the most precious thing of all and has got nothing in return. In 1967, the theologian Ratzinger asked: "Has not our theology in recent years often taken the same path? Has it not lowered step by step the claims made by faith, which were found to be far too burdensome? And always in such a way that nothing essential *seemed* to be lost, and yet always so much that one could soon venture upon the next step in the process?" At that period, he himself felt that these questions were too "global," but that they nevertheless got to the heart of the matter, since it was the treasure of the Christian faith that was at stake.

This was why he wrote his book: "It will help," he wrote in his academic style, "to promote a new understanding of faith as something that makes possible a genuine human existence in our world today. It will help to expound the faith, without transmuting it into a stream of words that conceal only with difficulty a complete intellectual emptiness."

In short, Pope Benedict XVI wants to reverse the barters made by Johnny: from nothing to the grindstone, from the grindstone to the goose, from the goose to the cow, from the cow to the horse, and from the horse to the precious gold, so that Johnny may once again be lucky. This is a difficult process, and an immensely demanding program for a pontificate.

Let the Faith Shine

Rather rapidly, the cardinals' tongues, so recently tied, were loosed in the first days after the conclave was over, and they offered their first answers to the question that people, Catholic and non-Catholic, were asking with increasing intensity all over the world. "Why had Joseph Ratzinger been elected pope from among them, by them?" Had a majority chosen the dean of the college as the new pope so that a conservative pontiff would preserve them from the reforms that were being demanded? Or did those who at first hesitated give their assent to Joseph Ratzinger because it was precisely he, as prefect of the CDF under John Paul II, who was best situated to know which changes could be acceptable to the tradition of the church and to its billions of members throughout the world? But wasn't everything already fixed in place? And wasn't this the work of Cardinal Ratzinger himself on such issues as the hierarchical structures *versus* a convinced or even a merely superficial democratization, celibacy and the prohibition of the ordination of women, sexual morality, and relationships to the other churches?

No one was better known to the 114 other cardinals than the German master theologian who had helped govern the church from Rome in the last twenty-three years. It was therefore somewhat surprising to hear the first comments of men such as Javier Lozano Barragan (a Mexican curial official) or Christoph Schönborn (archbishop of Vienna): they had not looked for a pope on the basis of previous achievements, like a committee evaluating candidates for a job on the basis of their experience. The main criterion had been what new energy a candidate could give the church through his own gifts and aptitudes, and what new vigor he could inspire among the faithful.

Even if the new pope was an elderly cardinal, he could still overcome stagnation, weariness, and frustration; this, however, could succeed only if a convincing metamorphosis allowed something new to emerge from the tried and tested tradition of the church. All the cardinals hoped that Benedict XVI would be a pope who would energetically take in hand the rudder of the bark of the faithful, beaten and tossed about by winds and waves—an ancient image of the church, which Ratzinger had evoked in his sermon on Monday morning. Collegiality was necessary, and the new pope would naturally work in this context, but without advocating for the church democratic models that had already proven inadequate in the secular world. The cardinals saw no need for a new ecumenical council.

They affirmed that we would now see the special character of the Petrine ministry in a new form, above all thanks to the pope's insistence on the specific nature of the church and to his tireless appeals to everyone of good will. The new pope would neither genuflect before modern society and its achievements nor reject these out of hand, and this balanced attitude would surely lead to a greater openness—one sign of which was the meeting with the press, which Benedict XVI announced for the coming Saturday.

What about "trials of strength" with the curia or with individual episcopal conferences? The question of power in the Roman Catholic Church seemed now to have received a definitive answer, which would hold good in the foreseeable future.

Spanish and North American cardinals felt that the time had come to turn their attention to the ministries within the community of faith, which were much more important, because it was within the church that the battle to preserve the central message of Christianity must be fought. It was their great hope that the theologian Ratzinger would help the Christian faith to shine with a new brilliance. This could be done only with the help of those who offered themselves selflessly for the service of the church, disregarding their own personal ambitions—and this applied not only to those who lived in celibacy, nor just to those who were paid full-time by the hierarchy.

As many of the cardinals said in public and private after the conclave, the Vatican organization seemed sufficiently well developed to cope with relationships between Rome and the dioceses; it was not necessary for the new pope to make refinements or improvements. On the contrary, it would be better for him to use his supreme authority to decree that the power of Rome should not become disproportionately great. The links to Rome are evaluated variously in the universal church, and the Vatican offices ought to pay more attention to this fact. Here too, the cardinals believed, Benedict XVI could relax a number of tensions, since no one was better acquainted than the new pope with the "nuts and bolts" of the Vatican. He would not take an exaggerated view of the importance of external structures but would focus on how the Vatican administration actually worked. This was presumably why the German pope initially confirmed all the curial heads of department in their offices; this was a reassuring measure that left future developments open.

Cardinals also told me that more and more laypersons in the worldwide church were carrying out apostolic tasks—not priests or members of religious orders—and working in the social and pastoral sectors, both in Western societies and in the southern hemisphere. Apart from questions connected with their salaries, permanent and reliable structures must be established to help them in their work. Even more importantly, they must be united to the church out of interior conviction and unconditional dedication, not merely as paid employees. These laypersons do not want to be clerics or religious in the traditional sense, nor do they want the rights and duties attached to those states of life. They must be helped to avoid careerist ambitions. Cardinals needed to find an ecclesiological status that is "neither fish nor fowl" (neither clergy nor simply lay persons), one that allows them truly to be themselves. This task cannot be put off indefinitely.

Almost everywhere in the world, there are communities with a spiritual profile, making fruitful contributions of various kinds to the life of the church. According to some cardinals who supported these movements of the faithful, these communities have often worked in secret because they do not fit the pattern beloved by the mass media, who like to report conflicts and controversies as a matter of "rebels bearing the Spirit of God and full of good will" versus "the rigid institution." Here, the cardinals agreed, we must support movements that take quite new paths. At the same time, we must encourage the religious orders of men and women: they are believing Christians who lead a common life, and they need a renewal that can be sought not least in the rediscovery of forgotten elixirs in their own history. As the Bible says, branches of the vine that have ceased to bear fruit are useless and dead.

The question of the ordination of women has already been answered by prefect Ratzinger with an almost infallible prohibition. But he will soon have to liberate this question from an obsession with the ordination to the priestly ministry. The cardinals did not elect him pope because they thought that he would permit the ordination of women; he had already stated that those Protestant churches that had ordained women to their ministry had not experienced any great renewal as a result. Benedict XVI will more likely be inclined to support the sisters of Blessed Teresa of Calcutta and similar selfless initiatives. Nevertheless, he has to convince people on this point: it is not enough to issue decrees.

The tensions in the worldwide church are growing, as cultural, societal, national, and regional differences increase, and many cardinals were convinced that a new pope must possess the gift of an authority that unites people. In the past, the unifying power of the Catholic Church has worked through the structures of papal authority and episcopal collegiality. The solidarity of Catholics has been demonstrated not least through their willingness to help each other in financial terms: for example, the Western churches, especially the German dioceses, have contributed huge sums to the church in the Third World. This is not a matter of a merely human compassion, nor did it happen by chance: it is the conscious expression of Catholic (and Roman) endeavors to promote a genuine unity within the worldwide church.

All the tensions and problems ought to have dissolved the Catholic Church a long time ago, and all the analyses of political science, sociology, and group dynamics suggest that such a dissolution would be inevitable—were it not for the papacy, this Roman bond of unity. A good pope can demonstrate in his own person the advantages of the Roman Catholic system, and this is surely a source of joy.

When they reflected on all these questions that demanded

an answer, most of the cardinals were relieved that they did not have to shoulder this enormous task themselves.

Cardinals who had belonged to the minority, not supporting Ratzinger as pope, tended to say that Benedict should not rejoice that he had received the papal authority, with all its dignities and its burdens. Nor should he rejoice in his position as universal teacher, which appeared to equip him with superhuman qualities, such as infallibility. Rather, he should seek to embody new qualities in pastoral work and in the celebration of the liturgy so that others would imitate him. Efficient decision making and working structures were indeed necessary in order to reconcile the authority of the papal office with the concerns of the people of God. The bishop of Rome is called to be chief pastor and an exemplary servant of God, and it is here, the cardinals said, that the Catholic Church must return to its original "recipes for success," indeed to the very ground of its existence. Its success is not due to the fact that it is a powerful institution and has always taught the correct doctrine but rather to its desire to accompany people with its treasures of wisdom. And it has never forgotten—neither in the stillness of the confessional nor in the solemn splendor of a feast—the words its founder, Jesus of Nazareth, uttered about God.

And the old cardinals said: on this point, we await great things from the theologian Ratzinger.

The Festive Inauguration

Once again, the whole world was there when Benedict XVI solemnly initiated his ministry as bishop of Rome with a pontifical Mass celebrated on the great steps in front of Saint Peter's Basilica. Hundreds of thousands of the faithful took part in the ceremony, which lasted almost three hours—not only in Saint Peter's Square but down the Via della Conciliazione to the Castel Sant' Angelo and in the adjacent streets of the Borgo district down to the Piazza Risorgimento. Leaders of other Christian churches and of the world's religions were present, as well as delegations sent by governments on all five continents.

Inevitably, there was a certain sense of déjà vu. After all, we had been here before, just over two weeks ago when the world had taken leave of John Paul II in a solemn Requiem. The dying of a great man had moved millions of people, and the ancient Christian liturgy with its proclamation of the mysteries of the faith offered a message of consolation. That morning, the sermon of the dean of the college of cardinals, Joseph Ratzinger, had touched hearts when he pointed up to the window on the third floor of the apostolic palace and spoke of the window in heaven, where the death and life of the pope find their eternal reward.

Now it was the same Joseph Ratzinger—for the past five days, Pope Benedict XVI—who before the Mass began went down to the tomb of the apostle Peter in the basilica, where he inspected the modest beginnings of the papacy. He was almost alone down there in the gloom of the simple burial place, crowned much higher up by Bernini's baldachin, and higher still by Michelangelo's cupola. The cardinals in their precious golden chasubles waited above at the high altar. The protodeacon, Medina Estévez, who had proclaimed the *Habemus papam!* in several languages on April 19, took from a reliquary the pallium and the fisherman's ring, the signs of the authority and burden of the papal office. It was only after praying alone at the tomb of the first apostle of Jesus Christ (and first bishop of Rome) that the new pope joined the procession of cardinals through the basilica. Now he met the deacon who bore the Gospel book before him as a sign that this was the real "government program" of each pontificate. It was only then that Benedict XVI emerged onto the dazzling brightness of the square under a blue Roman sky and was greeted by the cheers of the crowd.

At the explicit wish of the new pope, the ancient intercessory prayers of the church began, the "Imperial Laudes," prayers with which the faithful had invoked the heavenly help of the saints for so many centuries. Their help was certainly needed now, at the beginning of the new pope's ministry.

Once again, as had happened sixteen days earlier, the mighty ones of the world were present—not so many of them this time, but still a large number. The Catholic king of Spain and his queen, heads of state and government from countries that were more or less proud of their Christian roots, leaders from Muslim countries and from countries where other world religions dominated. But the center of attention was not these men and women, but Georg Ratzinger, the pope's older brother. His care-lined face suggested that he worried about what might be in store for the new pope.

Benedict XVI had chosen the scriptural readings with care. The Gospel, from John 21, was an obligatory reading, since it (together with Matthew 16) is the basis on which the papal claims to authority and their obligation to "feed the sheep" of Jesus are based. The first reading had an ecumenical touch: "For God the Lord is an eternal rock!" Were not these words from the prophet Isaiah a reminder that the true rock is God himself, not primarily Peter—and hence a nod in the direction of the Protestant churches? The leaders of the other Christian churches, whether present there or listening elsewhere in the world to the liturgy, will have been pleased at this choice of reading. Nor was it by chance that the second reading, from the First Letter of Peter, began with the words: "So I exhort the elders among you, as a fellow elder and a witness of the sufferings of Christ as well as a partaker in the glory that is to be revealed. Tend the flock of God that is your charge, not by constraint but willingly, not for shameful gain but eagerly, not as domineering over those in charge but being examples to the flock."

In his sermon, Benedict XVI explicitly declined to set out a program for his pontificate. He had indicated some guiding principles when he spoke to the cardinals on the morning after his election, "and there will be other opportunities to do so. My real program of governance is not to do my own will, not to pursue my own ideas, but to listen, together with the whole church, to the word and the will of Lord, to be guided by him." The full text of his homily, with its exposition of the Gospel, is given below. He accompanied his text with gestures and smiles that led many people to draw the conclusion: the stiff, cold Cardinal Ratzinger has become a real pope!

The external signs of this new office were the pallium and the fisherman's ring bearing the name Benedict XVI, which the protodeacon and the cardinal secretary of state (as subdean of the college) put on the pope's shoulders and finger. The pallium is made of sheep's wool, 8.5 feet long and 4.3 inches wide. It took the form used in the first millennium; the popes of the second millennium, including John Paul II, had worn a much shorter and thinner version. The homily commented on the meaning of these two signs. Finally, the pope was given the book of the Gospels, which he held out in all four directions. This is the true contents of the Christian message, which the church must proclaim "to the ends of the earth," the good news of the death and resurrection of Jesus, the good news about sin and holiness.

After the Gospel was read in Latin, it was read in Greek, its original language. The promise of obedience to the new pope was taken by representatives of the cardinals, bishops, priests, deacons, religious—a nun took part for the first time—married couples, and children. This was a simple and moving ceremony.

Now the transformation of the curial cardinal to pope was complete. He gave the blessing *urbi et orbi*, to the city of Rome and to the world, and then traveled slowly in an open, unprotected white car through the crowd, who cheered more and more loudly as the bells rang out. He blessed the pilgrims on his right and his left—and there were many banners in the blue and white colors of Bavaria, and people in the traditional costume of his homeland. The pope took his time in this encounter with the faithful. At the beginning of the Mass, his face had been tense, but now he seemed relieved, and he smiled happily—in keeping with a word that had recurred again and again in his homily, "joy." This was a pope who could enjoy being with the faithful on a day like this.

In the church of Saint Peter he later received the congratulations of the heads of state at the high altar; he spoke with some for longer periods of time, with some just a few words. He seemed already to have been pope forever.

Homily at the Inauguration

Your Eminences,
My dear brother bishops and priests,
Distinguished authorities and members of the
   diplomatic corps,
Dear brothers and sisters,

DURING THESE DAYS OF GREAT INTENSITY, we have chanted the litany of the saints on three different occasions: at the funeral of our Holy Father John Paul II; as the cardinals entered the conclave; and today, when we sang it with the response: *Tu illum adiuva*—"Help him," sustain the new successor of Saint Peter. On each occasion, in a particular way, I found great consolation in listening to this prayerful chant. How alone we all felt after the passing of John Paul II—the pope who for over twenty-six years had been our shepherd and guide on our journey through life! He crossed the threshold of the next life, entering the mystery of God. But he did not take this step alone. Those who believe are never alone—neither in life nor in death. At that moment, we could call upon the saints from every age—his friends, his brothers and sisters in the faith—knowing that they would form a living procession to accompany him into the next world, into the glory of God. We knew that his arrival was awaited. Now we know that he is among his own and is truly at home.

We were also consoled as we made our solemn entrance into the conclave, to elect the one whom the Lord had chosen. How would we be able to discern his name? How could 115 bishops, from every culture and every country, discover the one on whom the Lord wished to confer the mission of binding and loosing? Once again, we knew that we were not alone, we knew that we were surrounded, led, and guided by the friends of God.

And now, at this moment, weak servant of God that I am, I must assume this enormous task, which truly exceeds all human capacity. How can I do this? How will I be able to do it? All of you, my dear friends, have just invoked the entire host of saints, represented by some of the great names in the history of God's dealings with mankind. In this way, I too can say with renewed conviction: I am not alone. I do not have to carry alone what in truth I could never carry alone. All the saints of God are there to protect me, to sustain me, and to carry me. And your prayers, my dear friends, your indulgence, your love, your faith, and your hope accompany me. Indeed, the communion of saints consists not only of the great men and women who went before us and whose names we know. All of us belong to the communion of saints, we who have been baptized in the name of the Father, and of the Son, and of the Holy Spirit, we who draw life from the gift of Christ's body and blood, through which he transforms us and makes us like himself.

Yes, the church is alive—this is the wonderful experience of these days. During those sad days of the pope's illness and death, it became wonderfully evident to us that the church is alive. And the church is young. She holds within herself the future of the world and therefore shows each of us the way toward the future. The church is alive, and we are seeing it: we are experiencing the joy that the risen Lord promised his followers. The church is alive—she is alive because Christ is alive, because he is truly risen. In the suffering that we saw on the Holy Father's face in those days of Easter, we contemplated the mystery of Christ's passion and we touched his wounds. But throughout those days we have also been able, in a profound sense, to touch the risen One. We have been able to experience the joy that he promised, after a brief period of darkness, as the fruit of his resurrection.

The church is alive—with these words, I greet with great joy and gratitude all of you gathered here, my venerable brother cardinals and bishops, my dear priests, deacons, church workers, catechists. I greet you, men and women religious, witnesses of the transfiguring presence of God. I greet you, members of the lay faithful, immersed in the great task of building up the kingdom of God which spreads throughout the world, in every area of life. With great affection I also greet all those who have been reborn in the sacrament of baptism but are not yet in full communion with us; and you, my brothers and sisters of the Jewish people, to whom we are joined by a great shared spiritual heritage, one rooted in God's irrevocable promises. Finally, like a wave gathering force, my thoughts go out to all men and women of today, to believers and nonbelievers alike.

Dear friends! At this moment there is no need for me to present a program of governance. I was able to give an indication of what I see as my task in my message of Wednesday, April 20, and there will be other opportunities to do so. My real program of governance is not to do my own will, not to pursue my own ideas, but to listen, together with the whole church, to the word and the will of the Lord, to be guided by him, so that he himself will lead the church at this hour of our history. Instead of putting forward a program, I should simply like to comment on the two liturgical symbols that represent the inauguration of the Petrine ministry; both these symbols, moreover, reflect clearly what we heard proclaimed in today's readings.

The first symbol is the pallium, woven in pure wool, which will be placed on my shoulders. This ancient sign, which the bishops of Rome have worn since the fourth century, may be considered an image of the yoke of Christ, which the bishop of this city, the servant of the servants of God, takes upon his shoulders. God's yoke is God's will, which we accept, and this will does not weigh down on us, oppressing us and taking away our freedom. To know what God wants, to know where the path of life is found—this was Israel's joy, this was her great privilege. It is also our joy: God's will does not alienate us, it purifies us—even if this can be painful—and so it leads us to ourselves. In this way, we serve not only him, but the salvation of the whole world, of all history.

The symbolism of the pallium is even more concrete: the lamb's wool is meant to represent the lost, sick, or weak sheep which the shepherd places on his shoulders and carries to the waters of life. For the fathers of the church, the parable of the lost sheep, which the shepherd seeks in the desert, was an image of the mystery of Christ and the church. The human race—every one of us—is the sheep lost in the desert which no longer knows the way. The Son of God will not let this happen; he cannot abandon humanity in so wretched a condition. He leaps to his feet and abandons the glory of heaven in order to go in search of the sheep and pursue it, all the way to the cross. He takes it upon his shoulders and carries our humanity; he carries us all— he is the good shepherd who lays down his life for the sheep.

What the pallium indicates first and foremost is that we are all carried by Christ. But at the same time it invites us to carry one another. Hence the pallium becomes a symbol of the shepherd's mission, of which the second reading and the Gospel speak. The pastor must be inspired by Christ's holy zeal: for him, it is not a matter of indifference that so many people are living in the desert. And there are so many kinds of desert. There is the desert of poverty, the desert of hunger and thirst, the desert of abandonment, of loneliness, of destroyed love. There is the desert of God's darkness, the emptiness of souls no longer aware of their dignity or the goal of human life. The external deserts in the world are growing, because the internal deserts have become so vast. Therefore the earth's treasures no longer serve to build God's garden for all to live in, but they have been made to serve the powers of exploitation and destruction. The church as a whole and all her pastors, like Christ, must set out to lead people out of the desert, toward the place of life, toward friendship with the Son of God, toward the one who gives us life, and life in abundance.

The symbol of the lamb also has a deeper meaning. In the ancient Near East, it was customary for kings to style themselves as shepherds of their people. This was an image of their power, a cynical image: to them their subjects were like sheep, which the shepherd could dispose of as he wished. When the shepherd of all humanity, the living God, himself became a lamb, he stood on the side of the lambs, with those who are downtrodden and killed. This is how he reveals himself to be the true shepherd: "I am the Good Shepherd . . . I lay down my life for the sheep," Jesus says of himself (John 10:14f.). It is not power but love that redeems us! This is God's sign: he himself is love. How often we wish that God would show himself stronger, that he would strike decisively, defeating evil and creating a better world. All ideologies of power justify themselves in exactly this way; they justify the destruction of whatever would stand in the way of progress and the liberation of humanity. We suffer on account of God's patience. And yet, we need his patience. God, who became a lamb, tells us that the world is saved by the crucified One, not by those who crucified him. The world is redeemed by the patience of God. It is destroyed by the impatience of human beings.

One of the basic characteristics of a shepherd must be to love the people entrusted to him, even as he loves Christ whom he serves. "Feed my sheep," says Christ to Peter, and now, at this moment, he says it to me as well.

Feeding means loving, and loving also means being ready to suffer. Loving means giving the sheep what is truly good, the nourishment of God's truth, of God's word, the nourishment of his presence, which he gives us in the Blessed Sacrament. My dear friends—at this moment I can only say: pray for me, that I may learn to love the Lord more and more. Pray for me, that I may learn to love his flock more and more—in other words, you, the holy church, each one of you and all of you together. Pray for me, that I may not flee for fear of the wolves. Let us pray for one another, that the Lord will carry us and that we will learn to carry one another.

The second symbol used in today's liturgy to express the inauguration of the Petrine ministry is the presentation of the fisherman's ring. Peter's call to be a shepherd, which we heard in the Gospel, comes after the account of a miraculous catch of fish: after a night in which the disciples had let down their nets without success, they see the risen Lord on the shore. He tells them to let down their nets once more, and the nets become so full that they can hardly pull them in; they catch 153 large fish, "and although there were so many, the net was not torn" (John 21:11). This account, coming at the end of Jesus' earthly journey with his disciples, corresponds to an account found at the beginning: there too, the disciples had caught nothing the entire night; there too, Jesus had invited Simon once more to put out into the deep. And Simon, who was not yet called Peter, gave the wonderful reply: "Master, at your word I will let down the nets." And then came the conferral of his mission: "Do not be afraid. Henceforth you will be catching men" (Luke 5:1-11). Today too the church and the successors of the apostles are told to put out into the deep sea of history and to let down the nets, so as to win men and women over to the gospel—to God, to Christ, to true life.

The fathers made a very significant comment on this singular task. This is what they say: for a fish, created for water, it is fatal to be taken out of the sea, to be removed from its vital element to serve as human food. But in the mission of a fisher of men, the reverse is true. We are living in alienation, in the salt waters of suffering and death, in a sea of darkness without light. The net of the gospel pulls us out of the waters of death and brings us into the splendor of God's light, into true life. And this is really true: as we follow Christ in this mission to be fishers of men, we must bring men and women out of the sea that is salted with so many forms of alienation and onto the land of life, into the light of God. Yes, the purpose of our lives is to reveal God to human beings. And only where God is seen does life truly begin. Only when we meet the living God in Christ do we know what life is. We are not some casual and meaningless product of evolution. Each of us is the result of a thought of God. Each of us is willed; each of us is loved; each of us is necessary. There is nothing more beautiful than to be surprised by the gospel, by the encounter with Christ. There is nothing more beautiful than to know him and to speak to others of our friendship with him. The task of the shepherd, the task of the fisher of men, can often seem wearisome.

But it is beautiful and wonderful, because it is truly a service to joy, to God's joy which longs to break into the world.

Here I want to add something: both the image of the shepherd and that of the fisherman issue an explicit call to unity. "I have other sheep that are not of this fold; I must lead them too, and they will heed my voice. So there shall be one flock, one shepherd" (John 10:16); these are the words of Jesus at the end of his discourse on the Good Shepherd. And the account of the 153 large fish ends with the joyful statement: "although there were so many, the net was not torn" (John 21:11). Alas, beloved Lord, with sorrow we must now acknowledge that it has been torn! But no—we must not be sad! Let us rejoice because of your promise, which does not disappoint, and let us do all we can to pursue the path toward the unity you have promised. Let us remember it in our prayer to the Lord, as we plead with him: Yes, Lord, remember your promise. Grant that we may be one flock and one shepherd! Do not allow your net to be torn, help us to be servants of unity!

At this point, my mind goes back to October 22, 1978, when Pope John Paul II began his ministry here in Saint Peter's Square. His words on that occasion constantly echo in my ears: "Do not be afraid! Open wide the doors for Christ!" The pope was addressing the mighty, the powerful of this world, who feared that Christ might take away something of their power if they were to let him in, if they were to allow the faith to be free. Yes, he certainly would have taken something away from them: the dominion of corruption, the manipulation of law, and the freedom to do as they pleased. But he would not have taken away anything that pertains to human freedom or dignity or to the building of a just society.

The pope was also speaking to everyone, especially the young. Are we not perhaps all afraid in some way? If we let Christ enter fully into our lives, if we open ourselves totally to him, are we not afraid that he might take something away from us? Are we not perhaps afraid to give up something significant, something unique, something that makes life so beautiful? Do we not then risk ending up diminished and deprived of our freedom? And once again the pope said: No! If we let Christ into our lives, we lose nothing, nothing, absolutely nothing of what makes life free, beautiful and great. No! Only in this friendship are the doors of life opened wide. Only in this friendship is the great potential of human existence truly revealed. Only in this friendship do we experience beauty and liberation. And so, today, with great strength and great conviction, on the basis of a long personal experience of life, I say to you, dear young people: Do not be afraid of Christ! He takes nothing away, and he gives you everything. When we give ourselves to him, we receive a hundred-fold in return. Yes, open, open wide the doors to Christ—and you will find true life. Amen.

First Steps

When Pope Benedict's heart tells him to do something, he does it at once; and when his intellect tells him to do something, he does it even sooner. And so he decided, only four days after his election as pope and even before the solemn Mass of inauguration, to cultivate good relations with the journalists who represented the mass communications media. Some reported that he would be holding a press conference, but this was not the case. It was scarcely necessary; there has surely never been a new pope whose thinking on questions of theology and church politics was so well known as that of Benedict XVI.

The new pope conducted his meeting with about five thousand journalists in the huge audience hall on the Saturday morning, in a professional manner free of any nervousness. He spoke for twenty minutes in a number of languages, and although this was a short address, it was certainly substantial. He exhorted the journalists above all to respect human dignity in their own work—not just to remind other people to do so. Benedict XVI spoke critically of the "tyranny of the media," but he also thanked the journalists for performing in recent weeks "a service to the church."

On the Monday after his inauguration, the German pope met his fellow countrymen in the audience hall. It was a colorful, joyful, and moving occasion. Thousands had turned up to this first meeting with the pope, pilgrims and curious visitors from the German-speaking countries. They have a reputation for punctuality, but they accepted the late arrival of the new pope, who apologized and said that he had been "somewhat Italianized" by his twenty-three years in Italy.

He had a serious reason for being late: he had just received the representatives of other Christian churches and communities and the representatives of the world's great religions in the Clementine Hall in the Vatican. They had come to Rome for his solemn inaugural Mass, and the pope emphasized in words that came straight from his heart his commitment "at the start of my pontificate to total Christian unity, to the fellowship of all Christians in Christ." He saw the participation of the separated brethren at the Requiem for John Paul II and at his own Mass on Sunday as "more than just a simple act of courtesy." He asked the "dear friends of other religious traditions" who were present, including the Muslims, to build bridges of friendship in view of a better mutual understanding and an exchange of spiritual views. Peace was the duty of all human beings but in a special way of those who belonged to religious fellowships.

He left the Vatican and crossed the street to his old apartment on the Piazza della Città Leonina, where he met his older brother, Georg. His first official engagement outside the Vatican was a visit on the Monday evening to the patriarchal basilica of Saint Paul's outside the Walls, where the apostle of the Gentiles was buried. This visit had an ecumenical significance in the eyes of all who wished to see the hierarchical Petrine ministry complemented by the spirit of Paul, the apostle who wrote to the Galatians that he was once obliged "to withstand Peter to his face." Besides this, the venerable basilica is entrusted to the Benedictine order, the oldest monastic fellowship in western Europe, which follows the rule of Saint Benedict—whose name the new pope bore.

The Joyful Exhortation

Following the tradition of his predecessors, Benedict XVI held a public general audience in Saint Peter's Square for thousands of the faithful on the Wednesday after his inauguration. Under a radiant spring sky, the pope gave his catechetical instruction, first in Italian, then in French, English, German, and Spanish summaries. The English summary reads as follows:

Dear Brothers and Sisters,

IT IS WITH GREAT JOY that I welcome you and also greet those following this audience through radio and television. After the holy death of my beloved predecessor, Pope John Paul II, I come before you today for my first general audience. Filled with sentiments of awe and thanksgiving, I wish to speak of why I chose the name Benedict. First, I remember Pope Benedict XV, that courageous prophet of peace, who guided the church through turbulent times of war. In his footsteps I place my ministry in the service of reconciliation and harmony between peoples. Additionally, I recall Saint Benedict of Nursia, copatron of Europe, whose life evokes the Christian roots of Europe. I ask him to help us all to hold firm to the centrality of Christ in our Christian life: may Christ always take first place in our thoughts and actions!

I extend a special welcome to the English-speaking pilgrims here today, including groups from England, Wales, Ireland, Finland, Norway, Sweden, Australia,

Vietnam, India, Pakistan, Singapore, and the United States of America. Thank you for the affection with which you have greeted me. Upon all of you, I invoke the peace and joy of Jesus Christ our Lord!

The key concepts that the pope mentioned at the beginning of his pontificate were thus joy, peace, and reconciliation. He was seventy-eight years old, but he was intellectually active and seemed healthy and dynamic. His predecessor Benedict XV had lived in a world where differences of opinion between countries led to a bloody conflict; but it was the task of the popes then and now to exhort to reconciliation despite all the differences, to unity in peace. Both before and after the general audience, the new pope traveled unhurriedly in an open Jeep around the square. Once again, there was no armored glass to protect him. The atmosphere was festive, as it had so often been under John Paul II.

The Expectations for Reform

Will Benedict XVI be a reforming pope? Joseph Ratzinger was the chief guardian of the Catholic Church's faith under John Paul II, and he was elected by the cardinals because he was a theologian deeply rooted in this faith and possessing an excellent overview of the situation in the church. Can such a man initiate, support, and consolidate those changes in his billion-strong community, which the whole world seems to expect of him?

These reforms have been well known for some time now. In some instances, John Paul II made decisions about them; in

White smoke ascends from the chimney of the Sistine chapel, late in the afternoon of April 19, 2005.

Pope Benedict XVI on the central loggia of Saint Peter's Basilica after his election to the papacy. Many pilgrims had gathered on the Square to greet the new pope.

The name of the new pope is proclaimed.

Pope Benedict XVI greets the crowd.

Pope Benedict XVI greets the crowd from the loggia of Saint Peter's.

Opposite: Pope Benedict XVI on the loggia of Saint Peter's.

The pope appears
on the loggia,
while many
pilgrims greet
him from Saint
Peter's Square.

Saint Peter's Square during the
election of the pope.

View of Saint Peter's Square
during the inauguration Mass.

A married couple kneel before Benedict XVI.   Pope Benedict XVI blesses the faithful.

The fisherman's ring is placed on the Pope's finger during
the Mass on April 24.

Secretary of Benedict XVI.,
Georg Gaenswein

Bishops and cardinals on Saint Peter's Square
at the general audience, April 27.

Secretary of Benedict XVI.,
Georg Gaenswein

Bishops and cardinals on Saint Peter's Square, general audience, April 27.

Bavarian pilgrims on Saint Peter's Square.

The German press reported the election in detail, April 20 with the playful title "We Are Pope."

In Marktl am Inn, the Pope's birthplace, "Marktl Papal Beer" has been on sale since the election of Benedict XVI.

The pope's coat of arms: He is the first pope in modern times not to employ the heraldic the tiara (the threefold papal crown symbolizing worldly power). Over the crossed keys of Saint Peter is a miter. This change is probably intended to portray the pope's renunciation of worldly power and underline more strongly his role as bishop of the diocese of Rome and pastor of all Catholic believers.

Benedict XVI on the Vatican loggia.

The Hermann toy factory in Coburg produced a hand-made "Benedict XVI teddy bear" in a limited edition of 265 – Benedict is the 265th pope.

others, he refrained from making any decision, so that things remained as they always had been—in a world in which very little stands still anymore. Joseph Ratzinger had made his position on these issues known as a theologian, as cardinal arch-bishop of Munich, as prefect of the Congregation for the Doctrine of the Faith, and not least as dean of the college of cardinals, and in his last sermon before the election.

It is easy to make a list of what the whole world hopes the new pope will do. Benedict XVI is supposed to make the world a better place, prevent wars, defuse tensions between countries and peoples, abolish the yawning gulf between the poor and the rich, and cut back the explosive growth of profit-hungry capi-talism and every other ideology. His instrument in this work of reform will be the huge and powerful Roman Catholic Church with its "local branches," the individual dioceses. He must pro-mote justice and dialogue, peace and reconciliation. He himself has declared that this is why he chose the name *Benedict*. That would be a good continuation of the pontificate of John Paul II.

The reforms awaited within the church can be formulated somewhat more precisely. He must reduce the quantity of the magisterial teaching on sexual morality; indeed, he must stop uttering moral judgments that interfere in the lives of individu-als. For example—a primary concern in Western countries—he must allow Africans infected with AIDS to use condoms. He must allow women access to the priesthood, and abolish celibacy so that Catholic priests have access to marriage. He should open holy communion in the Catholic Church to the members of other churches and ecclesial groups; he should also lighten rules regarding divorced and remarried Catholics. He should give the laity, both men and women, more power in rela-tion to the clergy (who have dedicated themselves exclusively to the service of the church); for example, he should permit the laity to preach. In general, he ought to relinquish as much as possible of his papal authority and let the "people of God," as a democratic fellowship, take its own path. And not least, bishops and professors of theology should be chosen freely, without Roman intervention.

Many Christians, not only Catholics, will evaluate the new pope in light of this list of demands. If he does not fulfill these wishes, he will have failed their litmus test.

On all these questions, John Paul II held firmly and consistently to the traditional way of doing things, no doubt in the hope that some demands would become "superannuated" and imperceptibly disappear in the course of time. Cardinal Ratzinger helped support this ecclesial and political strategy, for a number of reasons. The chief of these was the fact that the pope, as the personified principle of unity, lays down the policy to be followed in the worldwide church, and this system has proved its worth down through the centuries. Why change it now? The wise Italian curial cardinal Agostino Casaroli, for many years the papal "foreign minister," once formulated this principle in a way that outsiders could never hope to understand: "If we err, we err along with the pope!" One may not agree with this at all; however, it does articulate one principle of the Roman Catholic Church.

Conservative in Principle

Even during the last pontificate, however, the cardinals, including Joseph Ratzinger, had pondered the question of what—theoretically speaking—*could* change in the Catholic

Church, granted the presupposition that something *should* indeed change. Here, it was not the critics' shopping list of reforms that argued in favor of changes but rather the simple fact that the church, in propounding its principles, not only faced the opposition of a wicked world but also the alienation of Christians of good will.

But what can the 266th vicar of Christ actually change, if the principle of the Roman church consists in being "conservative," in leaving the business of change to others while preserving with tenacity that which is tried and true? Today, this Roman principle appears reactionary and discredited; many people shrug their shoulders at so much rigidity and turn away from the church. And yet, this principle has prevailed since the end of the second century, and Rome knows no other way of conducting business. A new pope must accept this patrimony. It may be burdensome, but it also provides an orientation.

Whatever one thinks of this principle, it has certainly contributed to the success (if we may employ such a secular term) of the Roman Catholic Church. It is not so important whether a new pope is personally more or less conservative. He may even appear inclined to implement reforms. But the lesson to be drawn from the history of the papacy is that the bishops of Rome, with the cardinals who assist them in their ministry in the Vatican curia and in the various archdioceses, have become what they are because they adhered to tradition. In support of their claims to authority, the popes appealed to the unbroken succession of bishops of Rome from the very earliest period, who had handed on the Christian doctrine from one generation to the next. In this hierarchical institution, unity is not created by discussions that end with collegial handshakes but by affirming: "We have always believed this!" It is the novelty that is obliged to prove its worth, not the traditional way of doing things.

One may present theological objections to this ecclesiological model, but it will assuredly be difficult to convince the Roman church leadership—and Benedict XVI—that it is based on a misunderstanding. Even rebellious bishops accept this principle, once they have been created cardinals. Tradition is the source of the life of a church that has expanded beyond the city of Rome to embrace the whole world, and the pope recalls this fact every time he gives the blessing *urbi et orbi*, "to the city of Rome and to the entire world." This means that every proposition concerning faith and morals must agree with the tradition; only so can it win and maintain the assent of all the other regional and national churches. Others assure their survival and their domination by means of continual renewal and accommodation, but the pope holds the church together by means of his own immutability. It is in this way that he exercises the Petrine ministry of "strengthening his brethren." Peter is to be a rock in the storms that rage throughout the course of time.

Upholding the Tradition

If this analysis is correct, what does it mean for the many Catholics who suffer because of the problems they experience in their relationship to their church, or indeed for many other Christians and non-Christians? During the last pontificate, John Paul II was a particularly forceful embodiment of this Roman principle of unbending firmness in upholding tradition, despite his modern working methods, his communicative genius and his many journeys, his progressive views on social justice, and his insistence on the need for changes in the political arena. And this intensified the demand for reforms.

This firmness applied to the law prescribing celibacy for priests or to the admission to holy communion of the divorced and remarried or to the emphatic assertion of the impossibility of ordaining women to the priesthood—and indeed to a remarkable reluctance to consider anew the position of women in the church. On issues such as the regulation of births, contraception, or indeed everything concerning marriage and the family, and sex before or outside marriage, John Paul II refused even to countenance the questions raised in developed societies, and he was supported in this stony resistance by his chief theologian, who is himself now pope. Dogmas and moral principles were not toned down; on the contrary, John Paul II did his best, month by month, to cement them for the foreseeable future, in texts designed to remain valid for a very long time. Examples include the Codex of Canon Law, promulgated at the beginning of 1983, and the Catechism of the Catholic Church, published in October 1992 and binding on all the faithful. Since a codex or catechism is rewritten and subjected to the process of *aggiornamento* very seldom—only after centuries have passed—it seemed at the beginning of the third millennium, after the exceedingly turbulent pontificate of John Paul II, that the Catholic Church was condemned to a stasis, to an existence as a "rock" that would indeed be unshakable but would be increasingly isolated, since it would hurt the faithful, who would suffer because of its immobility.

On the other hand, many cardinals, bishops, and committed laypeople rejoiced, because they thought that this image of a church that had never changed and could never change was precisely what was needed today and in the future. In the long term, they thought this was the only way in which Jesus' promise to Peter could be realized: the gates of hell will never prevail against the church of Peter, the "rock" (Matthew 16:18—a text interpreted differently in other Christian communities). In a manner of cultural pessimism, Ratzinger had pointed out how many kingdoms and great institutions, how many promising cultural and religious movements had disappeared and had been utterly forgotten. This gave food for thought to even those cardinals and bishops who were favorably disposed to reforms, in view of the fact that the faithful in their dioceses were insisting that the time had come to change some things that had lasted for a long time.

In this light, then, the argument that modern Catholics will not follow ancient dogma and that the church needs to change in accord with a postmodern rational, democratic understanding of life lost its urgency. And in any event, Catholic tradition cannot be scientifically proven. The question now became whether a certain change would do more harm then benefit.

Faith as the Reason for Joy

What potential remained for reforms, if the dogmas and the essential principles governing human life were immutable? The writings of Joseph Ratzinger suggest that a great deal is in fact possible.

One central problem of the church is the relationship between the primacy of the pope and the collegiality of the many church leaders in the individual national communities. This was discussed forty years ago at the Second Vatican Council, which both confirmed the papal claims and stiffened the backbone of the bishops—although the bishops seem to have forgotten this, doubtless because of the sheer efficiency of the Roman machinery in recent decades. It is well known that the pope and the curia ("Rome") have centuries of experience and like to play the central role. But centralism is a problem in every global firm, and one notices a strange and unnecessary lack of imagination on the part of the diocesan bishops: why are they so reluctant to make use of the possibilities for creative action that they do in fact possess? And if they want to see changes, why do they not work toward the creation of a consensus in the world-wide church? They might well be surprised to discover that their colleagues share their views. In an age of universal communication, this is not an impossible task.

Some things can certainly change. The Catholic Church has painted itself into a corner with a number of its own decisions, and I cannot really see it living with the same complaints, year in and year out. For example, the canon law of the Latin church, unlike the Eastern churches that are united to Rome, has prescribed for many centuries that its priests must live in celibacy. The extent to which these prescriptions have actually been followed varies throughout history. There have been many lapses, but there has also been an exceptionally high success rate. Nevertheless, the Roman church must ask whether it is in its own interest to retain this law without any exceptions in every region of the world.

There are in fact exceptions already, for example, the priests of certain Eastern churches, or Anglican clergymen who (in some cases because they could not accept the ordination of women to the priesthood in their own church) have converted to Catholicism and have been allowed to exercise the full priestly ministry. Neither Paul VI nor John Paul II succeeded in halting the terrible erosion among the celibate personnel of the church in the last four decades; and the religious orders of men and women, with their voluntary acceptance of an unmarried life, have undergone an even more dramatic decline in numbers in the same period.

In a society in which sex is omnipresent, the mass media frequently wonder aloud whether celibate priests do actually live without sex. Many idealistic young men look on celibacy as a trap ensnaring them for life. And it is hard to see why priests who once had to give up their ministry because of the desire to marry, and have lived a good family life and done good work in their new professions, should not be allowed to return to the vineyard of the Lord, if they wish to do so. There are not so many men well versed in theology that the church can afford to exclude such priests forever.

Celibacy is, of course, connected with important goals in the Catholic Church, for example, that the priesthood should not just be one job among others; the renunciation of marriage has also been understood as a testimony to the values of the future kingdom of heaven, where there will be no marriage. This means that Benedict XVI will not be able simply to abolish this law. But he could surely increase the number of exceptions to the rule.

Celibacy is a prohibition that belongs to the realm of canon law, but John Paul II and Cardinal Ratzinger have affirmed that the exclusion of women from priestly ordination belongs to the realm of the truths of the faith. According to the practice of the church, it will take a long time to reverse this categorical assertion, since that would entail a break with structures in the church's work and life that a pope—for the reasons set out above—will surely wish to avoid. A change will come only if enough reasonable people persist throughout this century and the next in arguing in favor of opening ordination to women. At present, this seems impossible in a worldwide church that seeks inculturation in so many different regions. But perhaps the groups supporting women's ordination will one day succeed in demonstrating that their desire is in fact the work of the Holy Spirit, who wishes to transform a two-thousand-year-old practice. Benedict XVI will not change current practice with regard to the sacrament of orders, but he could try out new models, allowing women to take on a new role in the church. He is well aware that women—the Marian element, as Pope John Paul often said—are essential to the survival of the church.

There may well be changes in an area that is often thought of as "specifically Catholic," that is, moral doctrine concerning marriage and the family, the guidelines issued from the Vatican about "the human person as a sexual being." Here, the papal church is admired by some for its fidelity to its principles and dismissed out-of-hand by others as ridiculously antiquated. John Paul II gave an encyclical on moral questions the title *Veritatis splendor,* "The Splendor of the Truth," but he did not always succeed in demonstrating the beauty of that which is good and true. His vision of what human existence means was not always accepted, and a distorted understanding sometimes resulted. Here, it is not the elegant vocabulary of a Joseph Ratzinger that we need: in light of the previous pope's many words on this question, Benedict XVI may perhaps prefer to be silent.

The Catholic Church has survived for so long, unlike the various ideologies, because it has always respected the fact that human beings are genuinely a mixture of good and evil, and that they are both sexual and spiritual. Only a very few analysts of our age would deny that the ideologies of the Western societies are saturated by sexuality. Joseph Ratzinger would agree with this analysis. Even the best theologians have a tendency to put forward rigid propositions on the level of fundamental principles; the treasury of the church's experience and wisdom would suggest that he should tone down this rigidity. To begin with, he could simply keep silent about these principles; then he could open them up to discussion. Finally, he could concentrate all our attention on revealing the essential truths about human sexuality and the superiority of good over evil, even in this area of our lives.

This applies to the distinction made by Paul VI in *Humanae vitae*, his widely reviled encyclical about the transmission of human life, between "natural" and "artificial" contraceptive methods. The subsequent development of the medical, biological, and genetic sciences has made this distinction questionable. Naturally enough, Paul VI could not have known this in 1968, and he tied the church down unnecessarily when he affirmed that every sexual act must be open to the transmission of life. In view of the billions who throng our little planet, it must surely be possible to let human reason control the paths taken by nature.

For centuries, the Catholic Church had a flexible pastoral practice. Today, however, many who would willingly take an active share in its life find that the constant repetition of harsh moral doctrines makes them feel like pariahs—either in the church or in the wider society in which they live. This is true of people who have had traumatic experiences, have divorced and then remarried. This is true of homosexual persons. These "children of our time and of modern society" find it extremely hard to believe that there was once a time when the word

"Catholic" was associated with the joy of the senses and the full-ness of human life.

Joy in the faith is the all-pervasive reality in Joseph Ratzinger's life. He spoke glowingly of this joy in his first sermons as pope. If he is looking for an ambitious program for his pontificate, he might do worse than to try to bring this joy back into the church!

The New Pope and the New Catholics

The uninterrupted stream of thousands and tens of thousands, day by day, swelling soon to number hundreds of thousands and millions, was a fascinating phenomenon. It had already been experienced during the special Holy Year in 2000. And it had been repeated in past weeks while John Paul II lay dying, and then after his death—believers or merely inquisitive, old and young, often taking days for their journey, then standing in lines for hours on end in Rome.

It is not true to say that Cardinal Ratzinger questioned the religious quality of this stream of visitors. He is incorrectly reported to have said once that the church did not need young people who applauded the pope until they were hoarse, then left piles of used condoms behind on the meadow where he had celebrated Mass. It was, of course, true that he found it difficult to make sense of such paradoxes; it might perhaps have been easier if he had had grandchildren whom he loved, because he would have seen at first hand how they were struggling to make a synthesis of his "sacred teaching" and whatever is in fashion in modern society. They would probably concede that they often made a mess of the attempt, and he would ponder how he could help them—just as he had once self-critically reflected that a papal prescription, a "doctrinal note" of the Congregation for the Doctrine of the Faith, or a paragraph of the catechism was in fact meant to be "helpful."

Paris 1997, Rome 2000, Toronto 2002: these were the most recent World Youth Days for Catholics ages fifteen to thirty-five. The next gathering would be at Cologne on the Rhine in August, 2005. But now we were in Rome in April, 2005, and millions, old and young, were flocking to see Benedict XVI. The individuals in these crowds, irrespective of the nation and culture from which they came, found it completely natural to belong to one and the same church under this Roman bishop. They joined in praying the creed, their own profession of faith, formulated by the councils of the earliest Christian centuries, and spoke of the "one, holy, catholic, and apostolic church." They are not perturbed by any "difficulties" they might have with this church: they belong to it, and they are proud of the fact!

Do these people, these believing Christians, live in another age, on another planet, one around which the sun circles? Have they dropped out of modern life for the space of a brief visit to Rome? And will they then return to their ordinarily lives? Will these young people simply ignore the pope's sermons about sexual morality? If they are politicians, will they affirm that the highest of dogmas is the necessity of getting a majority in the forthcoming democratic elections? If they are scientists, will they hold that whatever can be done should be done? If they are intellectuals, will they assert the equal rights of absolutely every idea?

As cardinal, Ratzinger reflected uneasily on this dichotomy in modern Catholics; as pope, Benedict opens wide his arms and proclaims that these are his flock, whom he and the other shepherds must feed. They are perfectly normal people whom we could call the *new Catholics*, who are devoted to the church.

"New," because after the birth pangs of recent decades, they are displaying and practicing a new form of Catholicism.

They embody the wonderful image of the church as the "pilgrim people of God," evoked by the bishops at the Second Vatican Council, as they throng to Rome from north and south, east and west. We no longer see a church that is a rigid hierarchical pyramid, with the ministries of pope and bishop cemented firmly in place, with some who are higher in rank and some who are lower. What we see now is a fellowship of equals, endowed with the universal priesthood, each one raised up by sharing in the common holiness of God's people, as the New Testament teaches.

This powerful image of the "people of God" had led since the Council—comparable in its eruptive power to the cultural revolution of 1968—to far-reaching demands for a "democratization" that would alter the church's fellowship under the pope. But the new Catholics are astonishingly untouched by all the reforming proposals that envisage an ecclesiastical democracy. Not that they despise the blessings of democracy in political life! It simply seems that they are consistently uninterested in changing the structures of the church to reassign authority and responsibility.

This is because they see their church not primarily as a laboratory for the construction of new formulas of the faith or as a context for experimenting with democratic processes where opinion is formed and power shared in a manner parallel to (only more loving than) secular society. They do not feel the Roman magisterium or the teaching office of the local bishops as a yoke imposed on them. They do not feel the need to protest against this painful yoke in the name of their own reflections on the faith and their moral decisions. Rather, the church's teaching is a North Star to guide them on their way, an anchor that holds them fast in the waves of life.

In all this, the elites among the new Catholics are perfectly well aware of the theological and moral problems. These problems lose some of their acuteness, however, when the Roman path to a solution is experienced as better than that offered by other Christian churches. Another factor is the ability of ecclesiastical Catholicism—celebrated with pomp in Rome in a setting of high cultural value—to concentrate the eyes of the participant on what is truly essential and to permit people to genuinely enter the religious sphere. It seems that these believers hold that there is something more important in their life of faith than democratic rules and liberal opportunities. They appear to be "postliberal": it is as if the debates in church and society in nineteenth- and twentieth-century Europe are largely irrelevant to or inconclusive for their own future in the wide world, whether they live in Africa or in Hollywood, in South America or Dallas.

Salt of the Earth

Does this mean that such Catholics are opting out of the modern world—perhaps because they cannot accept the challenges of the new age, from genetic technology to taking responsibility for their own lives? The new Catholics are not affected to any great extent by these problems nor by changes within the church. They follow a rule that has been observed in Christianity from the outset, namely the discernment between good and evil that the Bible teaches: this does not mean an unqualified enthusiasm for the world and every modern society, since here too there are scribes and Pharisees and much that can harm the human person. It means a patient waiting for the first fruits of the kingdom of God; it means living in convinced hope; it means being good Samaritans, who practice the true love of neighbor.

These new Catholics do not agree with the rebels of the 1968 generation, who were skeptical about a society that led a "false" life; nor do they follow more recent fads. Rather, they take to heart the balanced exhortations of the First Vatican Council in 1870: "It is completely false to assert that the church is opposed to the cultivation of the human arts and sciences. On the contrary, it supports them in many ways. It neither ignores nor despises the benefits they bring to human life." The new Catholics readily accept the advantages of the modern age and draw at the same time on the treasures of the church. Benedict XVI will have to get used to this—and he will certainly not react to the situation by locking up the church's treasures!

This makes the new Catholics refreshingly "postmodern"; it is as if they had failed to register the conflicts in European history about the relationship between Catholicism and the modern age, for these apparently mean nothing to them. They move freely in their own world, whether in eastern Europe or in the Caribbean, in North America or in South India. It would never occur to them that it is "unmodern" to have objections to genetic technology—an accusation often leveled against the pope and Catholic moral theologians. In the third millennium, science and its applications have become too problematical for anyone to run blindly in pursuit of whatever is labeled progress.

If these new Catholics are not particularly interested in conflicts within the church and structural reforms and do not want to be continually lectured by church leaders on such topics, what is their relation to the modern age, to the normal challenges of everyday living? What are their priorities? These are the "core dimensions" of the church. They celebrate the holiness of God, the source of religious fascination, and they take part in hour-long liturgies, whether they are believers or less convinced. The Catholic liturgy unfolds its spellbinding ritual not as an end in itself but as a means tried and tested over the centuries for escaping from inane chatter and sophisticated discussions, so that one can lift one's eyes briefly to heaven and gain some idea of God and of the eternal destiny of the human person. These Christians have voted with their feet against the universal inflation of words and the trivialization of language. They have much more confidence in the traditional symbols, in signs handed down from ancient times—signs that theology calls "sacraments," where a few words suffice to transmit a rich substance.

These new Catholics also seek membership in a community. This need not always be one of the "spiritual movements" that have kindled the Christian fire in so many countries in the world—the charismatic renewal, Cursillos, Sant' Egidio, the Focolare Movement, the Emmanuel community, Communion and Liberation, the Legionaries of Christ, Light and Life, the Neocatechumenate, or Opus Dei. But all these groups count on the conviction and the active participation of their members. Naturally, their numbers cannot compete with the traditional pastoral units of the church, namely, the dioceses and parishes. The new Catholics are not afraid to be *different* from other people, precisely because they are untroubled by the fact that they are *the same* as other people—all that matters is that they are allowed to be *Catholic!* This recalls Joseph Ratzinger's 1996 book *Salt of the Earth:* Their great concern is that the Christian salt should not lose its flavor by an enforced assimilation to modern society.

APPENDIX 1

Chronology of Joseph Ratzinger Pope Benedict XVI

1927   Born on April 16, Marktl am Inn, Upper Bavaria

1945–1951 Study of philosophy and theology

1951   Ordination to the priesthood

1953   Doctorate in theology

1954–1955 Stands in for professor in Freising, Germany

1957   *Habilitation*

1958–1959 Extraordinary professor of dogmatics and fundamental theology in Freising

1959–1977 Ordinary professor of dogmatics and fundamental theology at the universities of Bonn (1959–1969), Münster (1963–1966), Tübingen (1966–1969), and Regensburg (1969–1977)

1962–1965 Adviser to Cardinal Frings at the Second Vatican Council

1964   Member of the Rhineland-Westphalian Academy of Sciences

1966   Member of the Academy of Religious Sciences, Brussels

1977–1982 Archbishop of Munich and Freising

1977   May 28, episcopal ordination

1977   June 27, created cardinal

1981–2005 Prefect of the Congregation for the Doctrine of the Faith, president of the Pontifical Biblical Commission and of the International Theological

Commission; numerous offices held; membership and honorary membership in Vatican and international institutions

1984   Honorary doctorate of Humane Letters, College of St. Thomas, St. Paul, Minnesota

1986   Honorary doctorate of the Catholic University of Lima (Peru)

1986–1992 President of the Preparatory Commission for the Catechism of the Catholic Church

1987   Honorary doctorate of the Catholic University of Eichstätt (Germany)

1988   Honorary doctorate of the Catholic University of Lublin (Poland)

1991   Member of the European Academy of Science and Arts, Salzburg

1992   Member of the Academy of Moral and Political Sciences of the Institute of France (Académie française), Paris

1993   Cardinal bishop

1998   Honorary doctorate of the University of Navarra, Pamplona (Spain)

1998   Subdean of the college of cardinals

1999   Honorary doctorate of jurisprudence of the University of Maria SS. Assunta, Rome

2000   Honorary doctorate of the Pontifical Theological Faculty of Wroclaw (Breslau, Poland)

2001   Member of the Pontifical Academy of Science

2002–2005 Dean of the college of cardinals

2005   April 19, elected pope; April 24, solemn beginning of Petrine ministry

APPENDIX 2

Cardinal Ratzinger's Sermon at the Requiem of John Paul II

"FOLLOW ME!" The risen Lord says these words to Peter. They are his last words to this disciple, chosen to shepherd his flock. "Follow me!"—this lapidary saying of Christ can be taken as the key to understanding the message that comes to us from the life of our late beloved Pope John Paul II. Today we bury his remains in the earth as a seed of immortality—our hearts are full of sadness, yet at the same time of joyful hope and profound gratitude.

These are the sentiments that inspire us, Brothers and Sisters in Christ, present here in Saint Peter's Square, in neighboring streets and in various other locations within the city of Rome, where an immense crowd, silently praying, has gathered over the last few days. I greet all of you from my heart. I greet the authorities and official representatives of other churches and Christian communities, and likewise those of different religions. Next I greet the archbishops, bishops, priests, religious men and women, and the faithful who have come here from every continent; especially the young, whom John Paul II liked to call the future and the hope of the church. My greeting is extended, moreover, to all those throughout the world who are united with us through radio and television in this solemn celebration of our beloved Holy Father's funeral.

Follow me—as a young student Karol Wojtyla was thrilled by literature, the theater, and poetry. Working in a chemical plant, surrounded and threatened by Nazi terror, he heard the voice of the Lord: Follow me! In this extraordinary setting he began to read books of philosophy and theology, and then entered the clandestine seminary established by Cardinal Sapieha. After the war he was able to complete his studies in the faculty of theology of the Jagiellonian University of Krakow. How often, in his letters to priests and in his autobiographical books, has he spoken to us about his priesthood, to which he was ordained on November 1, 1946. In these texts he interprets his priesthood with particular reference to three sayings of the Lord. First: "You did not choose me, but I chose you. And I appointed you to go and bear fruit, fruit that will last" (John 15:16). The second saying is: "The good shepherd lays down his life for the sheep" (John 10:11). And then: "As the Father has loved me, so I have loved you; abide in my love" (John 15:9). In these three sayings we see the heart and soul of our Holy Father. He really went everywhere, untiringly, in order to bear fruit, fruit that lasts. *Rise, Let Us Be on Our Way!* is the title of his next-to-last book. "Rise, let us be on your way!"—with these words he roused us from a lethargic faith, from the sleep of the disciples of both yesterday and today. "Rise, let us be on our way!" he continues to say to us even today. The Holy Father was a priest to the last, for he offered his life to God for his flock and for the entire human family, in a daily self-oblation for the service of the church, especially amid the sufferings of his final months. And in this way he became one with Christ, the Good Shepherd, who loves his sheep. Finally, "abide in my love": the Pope who tried to meet everyone, who had an ability to forgive and to open his heart to all, tells us once again today, with these words of the Lord, that by abiding in the love of Christ we learn, at the school of Christ, the art of true love.

Follow me! In July, 1958, the young priest Karol Wojtyla began a new stage in his journey with the Lord and in the footsteps of the Lord. Karol had gone to the Masuri lakes for his usual vacation, along with a group of young people who loved canoeing. But he brought with him a letter inviting him to call on the primate of Poland, Cardinal Wyszyński. He could guess the purpose of the meeting: he was to be appointed as the auxiliary bishop of Krakow. Leaving the academic world, leaving this challenging engagement with young people, leaving the great intellectual endeavor of striving to understand and interpret the mystery of that creature which is the human person and of communicating to today's world the Christian interpretation of our being—all this must have seemed to him like losing his very self, losing what had become the very human identity of this young priest. Follow me—Karol Wojtyla accepted the appointment, for he heard in the church's call the voice of Christ. And then he realized how true are the Lord's words: "Those who try to make their life secure will lose it, but those who lose their life will keep it" (Luke 17:33). Our Pope—and we all know this—never wanted to make his own life secure, to keep it for himself; he wanted to give of himself unreservedly, to the very last moment, for Christ and thus also for us. And thus he came to experience how everything which he had given over into the Lord's hands came back to him in a new way. His love of words, of poetry, of literature, became an essential part of his pastoral mission and gave a new vitality, new urgency, new attractiveness to the preaching of the gospel, even when it is a sign of contradiction.

Follow me! In October, 1978, Cardinal Wojtyla once again heard the voice of the Lord. Once more there took place that dialogue with Peter reported in the Gospel of this Mass: "Simon, son of John, do you love me? Feed my sheep!" To the Lord's question, "Karol, do you love me?," the archbishop of Krakow answered from the depths of his heart: "Lord, you know everything; you know that I love you." The love of Christ was the dominant force in the life of our beloved Holy Father. Anyone who ever saw him pray, who ever heard him preach, knows that. Thanks to his being profoundly rooted in Christ, he was able to bear a burden that transcends merely human abilities: that of being the shepherd of Christ's flock, his universal church. This is not the time to speak of the specific content of this rich pontificate. I would like only to read two passages of today's liturgy which reflect central elements of this message. In the first reading, Saint Peter says—and with Saint Peter, the Pope himself—"I truly understand that God shows no partiality, but in every nation anyone who fears him and does what is right is acceptable to him. You know the message he sent to the people of Israel, preaching peace by Jesus Christ—he is Lord of all" (Acts 10:34-36). And in the second reading, Saint Paul—and with Saint Paul, our late Pope—exhorts us, crying out: "My brothers and sisters, whom I love and long for, my joy and my crown, stand firm in the Lord in this way, my beloved" (Philippians 4:1).

Follow me! Together with the command to feed his flock, Christ proclaimed to Peter that he would die a martyr's death. With those words, which conclude and sum up the dialogue on love and on the mandate of the universal shepherd, the Lord recalls another dialogue, which took place during the Last Supper. There Jesus said: "Where I am going, you cannot come." Peter said to him, "Lord, where are you going?" Jesus replied: "Where I am going, you cannot follow me now; but you will follow me afterward" (John 13:33, 36). Jesus from the Supper went toward the Cross, went towards his resurrection—he entered into the paschal mystery; and Peter could not yet follow him. Now—after the resurrection—comes the time, comes this "afterward." By shepherding the flock of Christ, Peter enters into the paschal mystery, he goes toward the cross and the resurrection. The Lord says this in these words: "when you were younger, you used to fasten your own belt and to go wherever you wished. But when you grow old, you will stretch out your hands, and someone else will fasten a belt around you and take you where you do not wish to go" (John 21:18). In the first years of his pontificate, still young and full of energy, the Holy Father went to the very ends of the earth, guided by Christ. But afterward, he increasingly entered into the communion of Christ's sufferings; increasingly he understood the truth of the words: "Someone else will fasten a belt around you." And in this very communion with the suffering Lord, tirelessly and with renewed energy, he proclaimed the gospel, the mystery of that love which goes to the end (cf. John 13:1).

He interpreted for us the paschal mystery as a mystery of divine mercy. In his last book, he wrote: The limit imposed upon evil "is ultimately Divine Mercy" (*Memory and Identity*, pp. 60–61). And reflecting on the assassination attempt, he said: "In sacrificing himself for us all, Christ gave a new meaning to suffering, opening up a new dimension, a new order: the order of love. . . . It is this suffering that burns and consumes evil with the flame of love and draws forth even from sin a great flowering of good" (pp. 189–90).

Impelled by this vision, the Pope suffered and loved in communion with Christ, and that is why the message of his suffering and his silence proved so eloquent and so fruitful.

Divine Mercy: the Holy Father found the purest reflection of God's mercy in the Mother of God. He, who at an early age had lost his own mother, loved his divine mother all the more. He heard the words of the crucified Lord as addressed personally to him: "Behold your Mother." And so he did as the beloved disciple did: "he took her into his own home" (*eis ta idia*, John 19:27)—*totus tuus*. And from the mother he learned to conform himself to Christ.

None of us can ever forget how on that last Easter Sunday of his life, the Holy Father, marked by suffering, came once more to the window of the apostolic palace and one last time gave his blessing *urbi et orbi*. We can be sure that our beloved Pope is standing today at the window of the Father's house, that he sees us and blesses us. Yes, bless us, Holy Father. We entrust your deal soul to the Mother of God, your Mother, who guided you each day and who will guide you now to the eternal glory of her Son, our Lord Jesus Christ. Amen.

APPENDIX 3

The Cardinal Electors, 2005

The college of cardinals is the highest governing body of the Catholic Church under the pope. The college comes together during a pontificate for "ordinary" and "extraordinary" consistories. At irregular intervals, the pope adds new members to the college. The distinctive color of their robes is red.

After the pope's death, it is the duty of the college of cardinals to elect his successor, but when they reach the age of eighty, they lose the right to vote in the election. This was decreed by Paul VI, primarily for reasons of human kindness: he wanted to spare the older cardinals the stress and burden of a conclave, and the younger cardinals the stress and burden of having to look after the older ones. The curial cardinals, that is, those who are heads of departments in the Vatican, lose their offices automatically on the death of the pope.

At the death of John Paul II, the college numbered 183 cardinals, 117 of whom had not yet reached the age of 80. This means that it is only the cardinals under 80 who form the real electoral body, although all the cardinals may take part in the "general congregations," in which there is an open and passionate exchange of views about practical matters—but above all, about the *status ecclesiae*, the situation of the church in today's world. Two electors, the retired archbishop of Manila (Philippines), Jaime Sin, and the retired archbishop of Monterrey (Mexico), Adolfo A. Suárez Rivera, were prevented by illness from taking part. Hence, 115 cardinals entered the conclave on April 18, 2005.

The rank of the cardinals is precisely regulated according to the date of their creation and also according to the place they occupy on the pope's list for that consistory, and, finally, according to the "order" to which they belong. The highest in rank are the six cardinal bishops. Most are cardinal priests, pastors in the great archdioceses or dioceses scattered across the world; those who have no diocese are cardinal deacons: most of these work in the Roman curia, while others (e.g., Avery Dulles in the United States) are created cardinals in honor of their theological achievements.

* indicates the date of birth, followed by country of birth
➤ indicates the date of creation

Agnelo, Geraldo Majella, Brazil, * October 19, 1933, Juiz de Fora, ➤ February 21, 2001, archbishop of São Salvador da Bahia.

Agré, Bernard, Ivory Coast, * March 2, 1926, Monga, ➤ February 21, 2001, archbishop of Abidjan.

Álvarez, Martínez Francisco, Spain, * July 14, 1925, in Santa Eulalia de Ferroñes Llanera, ➤ February 21, 2001, former archbishop of Toledo.

Ambrozic, Aloysius Matthew, Slovenia, * January 27, 1930, in Gabrje, ➤ February 21, 1998, archbishop of Toronto.

Amigo, Vallejo Carlos, OFM, Spain, * August 23, 1934, in Medina de Rioseco, ➤ October 21, 2003, archbishop of Seville.

Antonelli, Ennio, Italy, * November 18, 1936, in Todi, ➤ October 21, 2003. He became archbishop of Florence in March 2001, and is a friendly and modest man, with a heart for the poor and disadvantaged; his political statements attracted wide attention.

Arinze, Francis, Nigeria, * November 1, 1932, in Eziowelle,

➤ May 25, 1985. He is prefect of the Congregation for Worship and the Discipline of the Sacraments. He was ordained bishop at the age of thirty-two, and accordingly took part in the last session of the Second Vatican Council in 1965. He has performed valuable work as president of the Council for Inter-Religious Dialogue; as a Nigerian, he is familiar with the problems connected with Islam. (Benedict XVI appointed him cardinal bishop in April 2005.)

Bačkis, Audrys Juozas, Lithuania, * February 1, 1937, in Kaunas, ➤ February 21, 2001, archbishop of Vilnius, formerly in the Secretariat of State in the Roman curia.

Barbarin, Philippe, France, * October 17, 1950, in Rabat, ➤ October 21, 2003, archbishop of Lyons.

Baum, William Wakefield, United States, * November 21, 1926, in Dallas, ➤ May 24, 1976, former head of the Apostolic Penitentiary.

Bergoglio, Jorge Maria, SJ, Argentina, * December 17, 1936, in Buenos Aires, ➤ February 21, 2001, archbishop of Buenos Aires, one of the leading figures in the Latin American episcopate.

Bertone, Tarcisio SDB, Italy, * December 2, 1934, in Romano Canavese, ➤ October 21, 2003, archbishop of Genoa, long-time coworker with Cardinal Ratzinger in the Roman Congregation for the Doctrine of the Faith, a doughty fighter for the faith.

Biffi, Giacomo, * June 13, 1928, in Milan, ➤ May 25, 1985, for-mer archbishop of Bologna, a "conservative" with a friendly manner and a strong choice of words.

Bozanić, Josip, Croatia, * March 20, 1949, in Rijeka, ➤ October 21, 2003, archbishop of Zagreb.

Cacciavillian, Agostino, Italy, * August 14, 1926, in Novate, ➤ February 21, 2001, former president of the Administration of the Patrimony of the Apostolic See.

Carlos Gordó, Ricardo Maria, Spain, * September 24, 1926, in Valencia, ➤ November 26, 1994, former Archbishop of Barcelona.

Castrillón Hoyos, Darío, Columbia, * July 4, 1929, in Medellín, ➤ February 21, 1998, former prefect of the Congregation for the Clergy and president of the Pontifical Commission "Ecclesia Dei."

Cé, Marco, Italy, * July 8, 1925, in Izano, ➤ June 30, 1979, former Patriarch of Venice.

Cipriani Thorne, Juan Luis, Peru, * December 28, 1943, in Lima, ➤ February 21, 2001, archbishop of Lima.

Connell, Desmond, Ireland, * March 24, 1926, in Dublin, ➤ February 21, 2001, former archbishop of Dublin.

Danneels, Godfried, Belgium, * June 4, 1933, in Kanegem, ➤ February 2, 1983, archbishop of Malines-Brussels, lively, sometimes volatile, and open to the possibility of reforms.

Daoud, Ignace Moussa I, Syria, * September 18, 1930, in Meskané, ➤ February 21, 2001, prefect of the Congregation for the Eastern Churches.

Darmaatmadja, Julius Riyadi SJ, Indonesia, * December 20, 1934, in Muntilan, ➤ November 26, 1994, archbishop of Jakarta.

De Giorgi, Salvatore, Italy, * September 6, 1930, in Vernole, ➤ February 21, 1998, archbishop of Palermo, a committed pastor of his priests and faithful.

Dias, Ivan, India, * April 14, 1936, ➤ February 21, 2001, archbishop of Mumbai (Bombay) with long experience in the Vatican diplomatic service; a man who knows the world political scene and the problems of Asia.

Egan, Edward Michael, United States, * April 2, 1932, in Oak Park, ➤ February 21 2001, archbishop of New York.

Erdö, Péter, Hungary, * June 25, 1952, in Budapest, ➤ October 21, 2003, archbishop of Esztergom-Budapest.

Errázuriz Ossa, Francisco Javier, Chile, * September 5, 1933, in Santiago de Chile, ➤ February 21, 2001, archbishop of Santiago de Chile, a member of the Schönstatt movement, with experience working in the Roman curia.

Etsou-Nzabi-Bamungwabi, Frédéric, CICM, Democratic Republic of Congo (formerly Zaire), * December 3, 1930, in Mazalonga, ➤ June 28, 1991, archbishop of Kinshasa.

Falcão, José Freire, Brazil, * October 23, 1925, in Ererê, ➤ June 28, 1988, former archbishop of Brasilia.

George, Francis Eugene, OMI, United States, * January 1, 1937, in Chicago, ➤ February 21, 1998, archbishop of Chicago, a leader among the U.S. bishops.

Giordano, Michele, Italy, * September 26, 1930, in Sant' Arcangelo, ➤ June 28, 1988, archbishop of Naples; family connections have led critics to question his moral integrity.

Glemp, Józef, Poland, * December 18, 1929, in Inowroclaw, ➤ February 2, 1983, archbishop of Gniezno and of Warsaw, "vicar" of John Paul II in his role as primate of Poland.

Grocholewski, Zenon, Poland, * October 11, 1939, in Bródki, ➤ February 21, 2001, prefect of the Congregation of Catholic Education, a respected curial cardinal.

Hamao, Stephen Fumio, Japan, * March 9, 1930, in Tokyo, ➤ October 21, 2003, president of the Pontifical Council for Migrants.

Herranz, Julián, Spain, * March 31, 1930, in Barcelona, ➤ October 21, 2003, president of the Pontifical Council for the Interpretation of Texts of Canon Law.

Hummes, Claudio, OFM, Brazil, * August 8, 1934, Montenegro, ➤ February 21, 2001, archbishop of São Paulo; as a Franciscan, he stands in the theological tradition of a spirituality of poverty. He is familiar with social and ecclesial problems, and is aware of their bearing on his pastoral ministry.

Husar, Lubomyr, Ukraine, * February 26, 1933, in Lwow, ➤ February 21, 2001, Ukrainian Archbishop Major of Lwow.

Jaworski, Marian, Ukraine, * August 2, 1926, in Lwow, ➤ February 21, 2001, Latin archbishop of Lwow.

Kasper, Walter, Germany, * March 5, 1933, in Heidenheim/ Brenz, ➤ February 21, 2001, president of the Pontifical Council for Christian Unity, a man whose commitment to Christian unity is based on theological conviction. From his Roman office, he takes a realistic view of the possibilities and limitations of ecumenical work.

Keeler, William Henry, United States, * March 4, 1931, in San Antonio, ➤ November 26, 1994, archbishop of Baltimore.

Kitbunchu, Michael Michai, Thailand, * January 25, 1929, in Samphran, ➤ February 2, 1983, archbishop of Bangkok.

Law, Bernard Francis, Mexico, * November 4, 1931, in Torreón, ➤ May 25, 1985, former Archbishop of Boston. Pedophile crimes committed by priests in his archdiocese led to a grave crisis in the American church and ended his ministry in Boston before he reached retirement age; today, he is archpriest of St. Mary Major in Rome.

Lehmann, Karl, Germany, * May 16, 1936, in Sigmaringen, ➤ February 21, 2001, bishop of Mainz and chairman of the German Episcopal Conference; a pragmatic man who seeks a solution to the problems of the Catholic Church in modern society.

López Rodríguez, Nicolás de Jésus, Dominican Republic, * October 31, 1936, in Barranca, ➤ June 28, 1991, archbishop of Santo Domingo.

López Trujillo, Alfonso, Columbia, * November 8, 1935, in Villahermosa, ➤ February 2, 1983, president of the Pontifical Council for the Family; a conservative who asserts his views energetically.

Lozano Barragán, Javier, Mexico, * January 26, 1933, in Toluca,

➤ October 21, 2003, president of the Pontifical Council for Pastoral Care of the Sick.

Lustiger, Jean-Marie, France, * September 17, 1926, in Paris, ➤ February 2, 1983, former archbishop of Paris; his conversion from the Jewish faith to Catholicism, his ecclesiastical career, and his intellectual brilliance set him apart.

Macharski, Franciszek, Poland, * May 20, 1927, in Krakow, ➤ June 30, 1979, archbishop of Krakow, a close associate and genuine friend of John Paul II, whose inheritance he upholds on questions of church politics.

Mahony, Roger Michael, United States, * February 27, 1936, in Hollywood, ➤ June 28, 1991, archbishop of Los Angeles, aware of the problems of the modern world.

Maida, Adam Joseph, United States, * March 18, 1930, in East Vandergift, ➤ November 26, 1994, archbishop of Detroit.

Marchisano, Francesco, Italy, * June 25, 1929, in Racconigi, ➤ October 21, 2003, archpriest of St. Peter's Basilica.

Martínez Somalo, Eduardo, Spain, * March 31, 1927, in Baños de Río Tobía, ➤ June 28, 1988, camerlengo of the Holy Roman Church. In the vacancy after the death of John Paul II, he carried out his important office conscientiously, namely, the preservation of the rights of the Holy See.

Martini, Carlo Maria, SJ, Italy, * February 15, 1927, in Turin, ➤ February 2, 1983, former archbishop of Milan. This Jesuit, who long headed one of the largest and most important dioceses in the world, is still highly respected after his retirement from office; he offers a convincingly genuine spirituality born of the spirit of scripture. From his new home in Jerusalem, he reminds the church continuously of its spiritual origins.

Martino, Renato Raffaele, Italy, * November 23, 1932, in Salerno, ➤ October 21, 2003, president of the Pontifical Council for Justice and Peace, a former Vatican observer at the United Nations who is well acquainted with world politics and was a keen supporter of John Paul II during the Iraq crisis.

McCarrick, Theodore Edgar, United States, * July 7, 1930, in New York, ➤ February 21, 2001, archbishop of Washington.

Medina Estévez, Jorge Arturo, Chile, * December 23, 1926, in Santiago de Chile, ➤ February 21, 1998, former prefect of the Congregation for the Sacraments.

Meisner, Joachim, Germany, * December 25, 1933, in Breslau, ➤ February 2, 1983, archbishop of Cologne, a conservative who is not afraid to utter vehement criticism of modern society, in season and out of season; a close confidant of John Paul II. He will play host to the World Youth Day in his cathedral city in August 2005.

Murphy-O'Connor, Cormac, Great Britain, * August 24, 1932, in Reading, ➤ February 21, 2001, archbishop of Westminster. He tackles the problems of his church and of his Catholics in England with a certain insouciance.

Napier, Wilfrid Fox, OFM, South Africa, * March 8, 1941, in Swartberg, ➤ February 21, 2001, archbishop of Durban.

Nicora, Attilio, Italy, * March 16, 1937 in Varese, ➤ October 21, 2003, president of the Administration of the Patrimony of the Holy See. His task is to keep the Vatican finances in order and to avoid as far as possible getting into the red.

Obando y Bravo, Miguel, SDB, Nicaragua, * February 2, 1926, in La Libertad (Chontales), ➤ May 25, 1985, former archbishop of Managua, with experience of the difficult socialist government of the Sandinistas and of the problem of liberation theologians. He has made his own contribution to peace and justice in this Central American country.

O'Brien, Keith Michael Patrick, Great Britain, * March 17, 1938, in Ballycastle (Ireland), ➤ October 21, 2003, archbishop of St Andrews and Edinburgh.

Okogie, Anthony Olubunmi, Nigeria, * June 16, 1936, in Lagos, ➤ October 21, 2003, archbishop of Lagos.

Ortega y Alamino, Jaime Lucas, Cuba, * October 18, 1936, in Jagüey Grande, ➤ November 26, 1994, archbishop of Havana since 1981, where he has had to endure the communist Fidel Castro as dictator.

Ouellet, Marc, PSS, Canada, * June 8, 1944, in Lamotte, ➤ October 21, 2003, archbishop of Quebec.

Panafieu, Bernard, France, * January 26, 1931, in Châtellerault, ➤ October 21, 2003, archbishop of Marseilles.

Paskai, László, OFM, Hungary, * May 8, 1927, in Szeged, ➤ June 28, 1988, former archbishop of Esztergom-Budapest.

Pell, George, Australia, * June 8, 1941, in Ballarat, ➤ October 21, 2003, archbishop of Sydney.

Pengo, Polycarp, Tanzania, * August 5, 1944, in Mwazye, ➤ February 21, 1998, archbishop of Dar-es-Salaam.

Pham Minh Mân, Jean-Baptiste, Vietnam, * 1934, in Ca Mau, ➤ October 21, 2003, archbishop of Ho Chi Minh City.

Poletto, Severino, Italy, * March 18, 1933, in Salgareda, ➤ February 2, 2001, archbishop of Turin, a zealous pastor of souls.

Pompedda, Mario Francesco, Italy, * April 18, 1929, in Ozieri, ➤ February 21, 2001, former prefect of the Supreme Court of the Apostolic Signatura.

Poupard, Paul, France, * August 30, 1930, in Bouzillé, president of the Pontifical Council for Culture.

Pujats, Jānis, Latvia, * November 14, 1930, in Nautrani, ➤ February 21, 201, archbishop of Riga.

Puljić, Vinko, Bosnia-Herzegovina, * September 8, 1945, in Priječani, ➤ November 26, 1994, archbishop of Sarajevo.

Quezada Toruño, Rodolfo, Guatemala, * March 8, 1932, in Ciudad de Guatemala, ➤ October 21, 2003, archbishop of Guatemala.

Ratzinger, Joseph, Germany: now Pope Benedict XVI.

Razafindratandra, Armand Gaétan, Madagascar, * August 7, 1925, in Ambohimalaza, ➤ November 26, 1994, archbishop of Antananarivo.

Re, Giovanni Battista, Italy, * January 30, 1934, in Borno, ➤ February 21, 2001, prefect of the Congregation for Bishops and president of the Pontifical Commission for Latin America, prized by John Paul II because of his optimism and his capacity for work. He is, so to speak, in charge of the "career ladder" of bishops and priests.

Rigali, Justin Francis, United States, * April 19, 1935, in Los Angeles, ➤ October 21, 2003, archbishop of Philadelphia.

Rivera Carrera, Norberto, Mexico, * June 6, 1942, in Tepehuanes, ➤ February 21, 1998, archbishop of Mexico City and the most important prelate in a country that is becoming increasingly significant within the Catholic Church.

Rodríguez Maradiaga, Oscar Andrés, SDB, Honduras, * December 29, 1942 in Tegucigalpa, archbishop of Tegucigalpa, a man who is both unconventional and pious.

Rouco Varela, Antonio María, Spain, * August 24, 1936, in Villalba, ➤ February 21, 1998, archbishop of Madrid.

Rubiano Sáenz, Pedro, Columbia, * September 13, 1932, in Cartago, ➤ February 21, 2001, archbishop of Bogotá.

Ruini, Camillo, Italy, * February 19, 1931, in Sassuolo, ➤ June 28, 1991, vicar general of the pope for the diocese of Rome and prudent chairman of the Italian Episcopal Conference; he seems withdrawn, but in fact has many contacts.

Sandoval Íñiguez, Juan, Mexico, * March 28, 1933, in Yahualica, ➤ November 26, 1994, archbishop of Guadalajara.

Saraiva Martins, José, CMF, Portugal, * January 6, 1932, in Gagos de Jarmelo, ➤ February 21, 2001, prefect of the Congregation for the Causes of Saints.

Scheid, Eusébio Oscar, SCI, Brazil, * December 8, 1932, in Bom Retiro, ➤ October 21, 2003, archbishop of Rio de Janeiro.

Schönborn, Christoph, OP, Austria, * January 22, 1945, in Skalsko (today: Czech Republic), ➤ February 21, 1998, archbishop of Vienna. This aristocrat is respected at home and abroad. He endeavors to secure balance and compromise, but he can also act decisively when necessary.

Schwery, Henri, Switzerland, * June 14, 1932, in Saint-Léonard, ➤ June 28, 1991, former bishop of Sion/Sitten.

Scola, Angelo, Italy, * November 7, 1941, in Malgrate, ➤ October 21, 2003, patriarch of Venice. A learned theologian, who knows the problems of church and society well and does not underestimate their seriousness. He supports the spiritual "movements" of committed Catholics.

Sebastiani, Sergio, Italy, * April 11, 1931, in Montemonaco, ➤ February 21, 2001, president of the Economic Prefecture of the Vatican.

Sepe, Crescenzio, Italy, * June 2, 1943, in Carinaro, ➤ February 21, 2001, prefect of the Congregation for Evangelization of the Peoples; a good organizer.

Shirayanagi, Peter Seiichi, Japan, * June 17, 1928, in Hachiōji, ➤ November 26, 1994, former archbishop of Tokyo.

Simonis, Adrianus Johannes, Netherlands, * November 26, 1931, in Lisse, ➤ May 25, 1985, archbishop of Utrecht.

(Sin, Jaime Lachica, Philippines, * August 31, 1928, in New Washington, ➤ May 24, 1976, former Archbishop of Manila, absent due to illness; played an important role in establishing democracy in his country, which is the only Asian land with a large Catholic majority.)

Sodano, Angelo, Italy, * November 23, 1927, in Isola d'Asti, ➤ June 28, 1991, cardinal secretary of state and hence "prime minister" under John Paul II. He heads the administration of the Vatican and therefore is very well acquainted with all the important persons and problems in the church.

Stafford, James Francis, United States, * July 26, 1932, in Baltimore, ➤ February 21, 1998, head of the Apostolic Penitentiary.

Sterzinsky, Georg Maximilian, Germany, * February 9, 1936, in Warlack (at that date in East Prussia), ➤ June 28, 1991, archbishop of Berlin, a respected pastor in the Catholic diaspora of the German capital, open to reforms.

(Suárez Rivera, Adolfo Antonio, Mexico, * January 9, 1927, in San Cristóbal de las Casas, ➤ November 26, 1994, former archbishop of Monterrey, absent due to illness.)

Szoka, Edmund Casimir, United States, * September 14, 1927, in Grand Rapids, ➤ June 28, 1988, president of the Pontifical Commission for Vatican City and of the Governorship of the State of Vatican City.

Tauran, Jean-Louis Pierre, France, * April 5, 1943, in Bordeaux, ➤ October 21, 2003, archivist and librarian of the Holy Roman Church.

Terrazas Sandoval, Julio, CSSR, Bolivia, * March 7, 1936, in Vallegrande, ➤ February 21, 2001, archbishop of Santa Cruz de la Sierra.

Tettamanzi, Dionigi, Italy, * March 14, 1934, in Renate, ➤ February 2, 1998, archbishop of Milan, with experience as secretary to the Italian Episcopal Conference and as archbishop of Genoa. John Paul II repeatedly emphasized that Tettamanzi was a man on whom one could rest one's hopes for the future.

Toppo, Telesphore Placidus, India, * October 15, 1939, in Chainpur, ➤ October 21, 2003, archbishop of Ranchi.

Tumi, Christian Wiyghan, Cameroon, * October 15, 1930, in Kikaikelaki, ➤ June 28, 1988, archbishop of Douala.

Turcotte, Jean-Claude, Canada, * June 26, 1936, in Montreal, ➤ November 26, 1994, archbishop of Montreal.

Turkson, Peter Kodwo Appiah, Ghana, * October 11, 1948, in

Wassaw Nsuta, ➤ October 21, 2003, archbishop of Cape Coast.

Vidal, Ricardo J., Philippines, * February 6, 1931, in Mogpog, ➤ May 25, 1985, archbishop of Cebu.

Vithayathil, Varkey, CSSR, India, * May 29, 1927, in Parur, ➤ February 21, 2001, Syro-Malabarese archbishop major of Ernakulam-Angamaly.

Vlk, Miloslav, Czech Republic, * May 17, 1932, in Lišnice-Sepekov, ➤ November 26, 1994, archbishop of Prague, with experience of communism, democracy, and atheism in modern society.

Wamala, Emmanuel, Uganda, * December 15, 1926, in Kampala, ➤ November 26, 1994, archbishop of Kampala.

Wetter, Friedrich, Germany, * February 20, 1928, in Landau, ➤ May 25, 1985, archbishop of Munich and Freising. He was professor of dogmatic theology before becoming bishop of Speyer in 1968, and is the cardinal with the longest experience at the head of a diocese.

Williams, Thomas Stafford, New Zealand, * March 20, 1930, in Wellington, ➤ February 2, 1983, former archbishop of Wellington.

Zubeir Wako, Gabriel, Sudan, * February 27, 1941, in Mboro, ➤ October 21, 2003, archbishop of Khartoum.

APPENDIX 4

Benedict of Nursia

Benedict of Nursia, Saint, feast July 11. Benedictine monasticism traces its origins to this hermit and abbot of late classical antiquity, who wrote the most important Latin monastic rule. He was born ca. 480 near Nursia (today's Norcia in the Abruzzi) and died on March 21, 547 in Montecassino. The date of his death is certain, but the year is only an inference from other sources.

Life

The main biographical source is Gregory the Great (*Dialogues* 2, wholly devoted to Benedict; 3:16; 4:7-8), but Gregory's intention was not to write a biography but rather to use Benedict as an exemplification of the mystical path to God. A radical interpretation could therefore go so far as to dissolve the historical element altogether, even denying the existence of Benedict; but such skepticism is inappropriate. At the very least, the stories of miracles demonstrate the high esteem that Benedict enjoyed in sixth-century central Italy as a *vir Dei*.

He came at a very young age to Rome, to study the liberal arts. After a *conversio,* he initially joined a group of ascetics in Effide (Affile) near Subiaco, and then lived for three years as a hermit in a grotto in Subiaco. He was abbot of a monastery in this region for a short period (there is no historical evidence for the assertion that this was Vicovaro); after this failure, he returned to Subiaco and founded twelve "monasteries" for the disciples who joined him. He left Subiaco with some of his monks between 520 and 530. According to Gregory, this was because of opposition on the part of the clergy, but it is more likely that the problem lay in the novelty of his conception of the monastic life. He founded a new monastery in the *arx* (citadel) of Casinum (Montecassino). He transformed a pagan temple that stood on this site into a church dedicated to St. Martin and erected an oratory of St. John on the peak of the mountain. Although Gregory does not mention this point, Benedict must have had authorization from the civil government (i.e., the Goths) to take possession of the acropolis, and we must assume that he received extensive gifts of lands, which formed the kernel of the later *terra S. Benedicti* of the monastery. It was only here, in Montecassino, that Benedict wrote his rule. The visit by the Gothic king Totila in the second half of 546 is the point of reference for the date of Benedict's death (the older dating to 543 was based on the symbolism of the number 14); attempts to date it to 550 or even later must be rejected because of the chronology of the abbots of Montecassino before it was destroyed by the Lombards in 577.

Veneration

According to the tradition of Fleury (the oldest account is from the eighth century), the bones of Benedict were translated to Fleury, and those of his sister Scholastica to Le Mans, in the period between 577 and the resettlement of Montecassino in 717. Until the beginning of the eleventh century, Fleury was the center of the veneration of Benedict. Excavations under the high altar of Montecassino in 1950 brought to light the skeletons of an elderly man and of a woman; the male skeleton and the bones in Fleury did not belong to the same body. It is impossible to decide the question of authenticity, but it is plausible to assume that the wrong bones of "Benedict" were taken to Gaul when the monks of Fleury stole the relics.

In 1964, Paul VI proclaimed Benedict patron of Europe.

APPENDIX 5

The Roman Popes and the Benedicts

It is the most difficult and the most ancient of inheritances, controversial and at the same time greatly admired, that anyone can take on: the office of pope. When a man is elected pope and says: "I accept," as Joseph Cardinal Ratzinger did when he was elected Benedict XVI, he must know what he is letting himself in for. This is emphasized by the various titles and functions that announce the highest of claims on the part of the man who holds this office—and at the same time provoke criticism and contradiction: "Bishop of Rome, Vicar of Jesus Christ, Successor of the Prince of the Apostles (Peter), High Priest, Supreme Pontiff of the Universal Church, Patriarch of the West, Primate of Italy, Archbishop and Metropolitan of the Roman Ecclesiastical Province, Sovereign of the State of the Vatican City, Servant of the Servants of God."

Nothing higher than this can be formulated; even today, the great and mighty ones of the world seem small alongside the holder of such titles, as was shown by the solemn Requiem Mass for John Paul II on Friday, April 8, 2005, in Saint Peter's Square, with more than two hundred heads of state and government from the whole world, with hundreds of thousands of people on the squares and in front of the churches in Rome, and with millions of the faithful and pious television viewers on all the continents.

And yet, it all began modestly with a few words, which according to the biblical tradition were spoken by Jesus of Nazareth, the founder of Christianity, to Peter, the leader of the group of his "sympathizers" and disciples. These words, in the Latin tongue, now stand in huge letters high up in Saint Peter's Basilica: "You are Peter, and on this rock I will build my church, and the gates of hell will not overcome it. I will give you the keys of the kingdom of heaven." These words are written on the tympanum in Michelangelo's cupola, high above the tomb of Peter, above the high altar with Bernini's baldachin. And around the lofty walls in the aisles of the church, scrolls carry Jesus' other words, the threefold hammer-blows of his summons to Peter: "Feed my lambs! Tend my sheep! Feed my sheep!" And those other words of the Lord: "Simon, when you have repented, strengthen your brothers." Whatever these words may originally have meant, however they may have been understood and interpreted in the course of the history of the Christian churches and communities, they remain the mystery of the popes, the myth of the papacy.

In his pontificate, which lasted over twenty-six years, John Paul II expounded this commission in his own way and displayed it to the whole world: in Rome and on innumerable visits to the parishes of the Eternal City, on his countless pastoral journeys in Italy, and on 104 apostolic journeys on all the continents. It was not his own message he was preaching but the message of Another. And that is perhaps the greatest mystery of the popes, indeed ultimately their profoundest "recipe for success." Between Peter and Benedict XVI, sometimes through dark and very somber times, lies the history of the papacy and of the popes, which is often identical to the history of Europe itself.

The Roman Popes

Peter	–67?
Linus	67?–79?
Anacletus I	79?–91?
Clement I	91?–101?
Evaristus	101?–107?
Alexander I	107?–116?
Sixtus I	116?–125?
Telesphorus	125?–138?
Hyginus	138?–142?
Pius I	142?–155?
Anicetus	155?–166?
Soter	166?–174?
Eleutherus	174?–189?
Victor I	189?–198?
Zephyrinus	198?–217?
Calixtus I	217?–222
Hippolytus*	217?–235
Urban I	222–230
Pontian	230–235
Anterus	235–236
Fabian	236–250
Cornelius	251–253
Novatian*	251–258?
Lucius I	253–254
Stephen I	254–257
Sixtus II	257–258
Dionysius	259?–268?
Felix I	268?–274?
Eutychian	274?–282?
Gaius	282?–295?

---

* An asterisk following a name indicates those who should not be regarded as legitimate bishops of Rome.

Marcellinus	296?–304
Marcellus I	307?–309?
Eusebius	309?–310?
Miltiades	310–314
Silvester I	314–335
Mark	336
Julius I	337–352
Liberius	352–366
Felix (II)*	355–358
Damasus I	366–384
Ursinus*	366–367
Siricius	384–399
Anastasius I	399–402
Innocent I	402–417
Zosimus	417–418
Boniface I	418–422
Celestine I	422–432
Sixtus III	432–440
Leo I	440–461
Hilary	461–468
Simplicius	468–483
Felix II (III)	483–492
Gelasius I	492–496
Anastasius II	496–498
Symmachus	498–514
Laurence*	498–507
Hormisdas	514–523
John I	523–526
Felix III (IV)	526–530
Dioscurus	530
Boniface II	530–532
John II	533–535
Agapitus I	535–536

Silverius	536–537
Vigilius	537–555
Pelagius I	556–561
John III	561–574
Benedict I	575–579

Benedict I (June 2, 575–July 30, 579). A Roman, whose pontificate, about which information is sparse, was hard pressed by the Langobard siege of Rome in 579. Benedict and the Roman senate looked to Byzantium for help, but because of the war with the Persians, its assistance was completely inadequate. Benedict consecrated twenty-one bishops.

Pelagius II	579–590
Gregory I	590–604
Sabinian	604–606
Boniface III	607
Boniface IV	608–615
Adeodatus I	615–618
Boniface V	619–625
Honorius I	625–638
Severinus	640
John IV	640–642
Theodore I	641–649
Martin I	649–653 (655)
Eugene I	654–657
Vitalian	657–672
Adeodatus II	672–676
Donus	676–678
Agatho	678–681
Leo II	682–683

Benedict II   683–685

Benedict II (June 26, 683–May 8, 685). Saint (feast day May 7). After his election (in the beginning of June 683), the consecration was delayed for a year, since confirmation of the election had to be obtained from Byzantium. Under the aegis of the peace between Byzantium (under Emperor Constantine IV) and Rome, future papal elections were to be confirmed once again by the exarch of Ravenna; and the autonomy of Ravenna (after the Monthelitism dispute) was abolished. Benedict worked for the recognition of the Sixth Ecumenical Council (Constantinople 680/681) in the West, especially in the self-confident Visigothic churches. He restored Roman churches.

John V	685–686
Conon	686–687
Theodore*	687
Paschal*	687
Sergius I	687–701
John VI	701–705
John VII	705–707
Sisinnius	708
Constantine I	708–715
Gregory II	715–731
Gregory III	731–741
Zachary	741–752
Stephen (II)*	752
Stephen II	752–757
Paul I	757–767
Constantine II*	767–768

Philip*	768
Stephen III	768–772
Hadrian I	772–795
Leo III	795–816
Stephen IV	816–817
Paschal I	817–824
Eugene II	824–827
Valentine	827
Gregory IV	827–844
John (VIII)*	844
Sergius II	844–847
Leo IV	847–855
Benedict III	855–858

Benedict III (Sept. 29, 855–April 7, 858). A Roman, Benedict was elected immediately after the death of Leo IV (July 17, 855), but in order to be consecrated he needed the consent of Emperor Louis II. An influential group, supported by the imperial ambassadors, denied him recognition and elevated Anastasius Bibliothecarius, who had been condemned by Leo IV, as antipope. Anastasius had Benedict imprisoned but ran into open opposition as a result. Benedict, a cultivated man intent on compromise, was consecrated, with the consent of imperial ambassadors, on September 29, 855, in St. Peter's. This confusion provided the starting point for the later legend of Pope Joan. Benedict treated Anastasius gently, strove for peace between Louis II and his brothers, and managed to strengthen papal authority vis-à-vis Patriarch Ignatius of Constantinople, Archbishop Hinkmar of Reims, and in England. The *Liber Pontificalis* praises his service to the churches of Rome.

Anastasius III*	855
Nicholas I	858–867
Hadrian II	867–872
John VIII	872–882
Marinus I	882–884
Hadrian III	884–885
Stephen V	885–891
Formosus	891–896
Boniface VI	896
Stephen VI	896–897
Romanus	897
Theodore II	897
John IX	898–900
Benedict IV	900–903

Benedict IV (May/June 900–July/August 903). A Roman, considered a member of the party of Pope Formosus. In 900 he held a Lateran synod. In February 901 he crowned Louis II as emperor, who subsequently was defeated by his Italian opponent, King Berengar, in 903. At this point the papacy was threatening to flounder amid the wildly partisan struggles of the so-called dark ages (*saeculum obscurum*).

Leo V	903
Christopher	903–904
Sergius III	904–911
Anastasius III	911–913
Lando	913–914
John X	914–928
Leo VI	928
Stephen VII	929–931

John XI	931–936
Leo VII	936–939
Stephen VIII	939–942
Marinus II	941–946
Agapitus II	946–955
John XII	955–964
Leo VIII	963–965
Benedict V	964

Benedict V (end of May–end of June 964). The learned Roman scholastic and deacon *Benedictus Grammaticus* was chosen by the Romans after the death of John XII instead of the banished Leo VIII and against the wishes of Emperor Otto I. But he was then handed over to the emperor, who was besieging Rome, and was formally deposed at a Lateran synod by Leo and Otto. He died in Hamburg on July 4, 965, supposedly just before his restitution, which the Romans had asked for. His body was transferred to Rome in 988 on orders from Otto II.

John XIII	965–972
Benedict VI	973–974

Benedict VI (Jan. 19, 973–end of June 974). Son of Hildebrand Monachus from the sub-Capitolean region of Rome. He was a (cardinal) deacon of San Teodoro before he was elected, probably as early as September 972. The enthronement did not take place until the emperor gave his consent. Only a few documents have been preserved from his pontificate. Among others, the confirmation of the diocese of Prague has been lost. He was overthrown by a revolt of the Crescentian clan, and in July 974, despite the intervention of an imperial envoy, he was murdered in the Castel Sant' Angelo on orders of Boniface VII.

Boniface VII	974–985
Benedict VII	974–983

Benedict VII (October 974–July 7, 983). The nephew of the Roman prince Alberic II and bishop of Sutri was elected in the presence of an envoy of Otto II. Many documents have been preserved from his pontificate, which was oriented to cooperation with the emperor and was shaken by Boniface VII and his followers. Among these documents are the confirmation of the German primate for Mainz in 975. In 981 a Lateran synod that had been arranged with Otto condemned simony. He also made important contacts with Spain.

John XIV	983–984
John XV	985–996
Gregory V	996–999
John XVI*	997–998
Silvester II	999–1003
John XVII	1003
John XVIII	1003–1009
Sergius IV	1009–1012
Benedict VIII	1012–1024

Benedict VIII (May 17, 1012–April 9, 1024). Formerly *Theophylactus*. As the second son of Gregory of Tusculum, he was elevated to the papacy as a layman; he managed to prevail against Gregory VI and was consecrated on May 21. In contrast to his predecessors he sought out contact with the German court, which led to his coronation of

Henry II as emperor on February 14, 1014. At a synod in Ravenna in 1014 both men took action against simony, as well as cooperating in other matters. After the uprising against Byzantium in Apulia, which he supported with Norman mercenaries, collapsed in October 1018, he arranged to meet with the emperor at Easter in Bamberg in 1020. In the same year the Privilegium Ottonianum was renewed. In the summer of 1022 the military campaign in southern Italy pursued its largely fruitless course. On August 1, 1022, both Benedict and Henry continued the councils in Pavia, which promulgated regulations against clerical marriage. Since 1014 there had been connections between Benedict and reform-minded circles around Abbot Odilo of Cluny. In the spring of 1016, with help from Genoa and Pisa, Benedict overcame pirates off Sardinia. He did not become involved in German disputes, except in the Hammerstein marriage affair. His pontificate was characterized by close cooperation with the emperor and an effort to strengthen the papacy.

Gregory VI*	1012
John XIX	1024–1032
Benedict IX	1032–1045

Benedict IX (Oct. 21, 1032–May 1, 1045). Formerly *Theophylactus*, the nephew of both his predecessors John XIX and Benedict VIII; a layman. With help from his father, Alberic III of Tusculum, he was elevated to the papacy in his youth (not as a child). He maintained a careful distance from the German royal court. In the dispute of Conrad II with Archbishop Aribert of Milan, he supported the emperor, but not until 1038 after a meeting in Spello. In the conflict between Grado and Aquileia he decided

(1044) in favor of Grado, contrary to German interests. Making use of family connections and a supple policy vis-à-vis Byzantium he succeeded in extending the Latin church in southern Italy. Contacts are known to have existed between Benedict and reform circles in Italy and France. Banished from Rome by a revolt of the aristocracy in September 1044, he expelled the antipope Sylvester III. On May 5, 1045, he abdicated in favor of Gregory VI in exchange for money paid to his partisans. On December 24, 1046, he was deposed in Rome by Henry III. After the death of Clement II he took up his pontificate again, but on July 16, 1048, he had to give way to Damasus II. A renewed attempt to seize power in April 1054 likewise came to grief. He supposedly died between September 18, 1055, and January 9, 1056, as a penitent in the monastery of Grottaferrata .

Silvester III	1045
Gregory VI	1045–1046
Clement II	1046–1047
Damasus II	1048
Leo IX	1049–1054
Victor II	1055–1057
Stephen IX	1057–1058
Benedict X	1058–1059

Benedict X (Apr. 5, 1058–Apr. 1059). Formerly *John of Velletri,* probably not the same person as Bishop Benedict of Velletri, who is mentioned in 1057 as belonging to a circle of reform-minded cardinals. After the death of Stephen IX, he was elevated to the papacy under the leadership of the Tusculans, but he was not recognized by the reform cardinals, who elected Nicholas II in December

1058 in Siena. Benedict was excommunicated in January 1059 at a synod in Sutri. He was banished from Rome and was forced, with Norman help, to submit in Galleria. He was deprived of spiritual honors by the Lateran Synod in April 1060; he died under Gregory VII (after 1073) in a Roman monastery.

Nicholas II	1059–1061
Alexander II	1061–1073
Honorius II*	1061–1072
Gregory VII	1073–1085
Clement III*	1084–1100
Victor III	1086–1087
Urban II	1088–1099
Paschal II	1099–1118
Theodoricus*	1100–1101
Albert*	1101
Silvester IV*	1105–1111
Gelasius II	1118–1119
Gregory VIII*	1118–1121
Calixtus II	1119–1124
Celestine (II)*	1124
Honorius II	1124–1130
Innocent II	1130–1143
Anacletus II	1130–1138
Victor IV*	1138
Celestine II	1143–1144
Lucius II	1144–1145
Eugene III	1145–1153
Anastasius IV	1153–1154
Hadrian IV	1154–1159
Alexander III	1159–1181
Victor IV*	1159–1164

Paschal III*	1164–1168
Calixtus III*	1168–1178
Innocent III*	1179–1180
Lucius III	1181–1185
Urban III	1185–1187
Gregory VIII	1187
Clement III	1187–1191
Celestine III	1191–1198
Innocent III	1198–1216
Honorius III	1216–1227
Gregory IX	1227–1241
Celestine IV	1241
Innocent IV	1243–1254
Alexander IV	1254–1261
Urban IV	1261–1264
Clement IV	1265–1268
Gregory X	1271–1276
Innocent V	1276
Hadrian V	1276
John XXI	1276–1277
Nicholas III	1277–1280
Martin IV	1281–1285
Honorius IV	1285–1287
Nicholas IV	1288–1292
Celestine V	1294
Boniface VIII	1294–1303
Benedict XI	1303–1304

Benedict XI (Oct. 22, 1303–July 7, 1304). Blessed (1736; feast day July 7), a Dominican (1257). Formerly *Niccolò di Boccassio*, born in Treviso in 1240, died in Perugia. He may have studied in Milan (1262–1268); he taught theology in Venice and Genoa; he became provincial of Lombardy

(1286–1289, 1293–1296), and General-master in 1296. From 1297 he obliged the order to follow the papal position; he was a member of an embassy to the kings of France and England. In 1298 he was made cardinal of Santa Sabina, in 1300 cardinal bishop of Ostia. He went on only modestly successful legations (Hungary, Vienna); in 1303 after a brief conclave dominated by the pro-Boniface cardinal Matteo Rosso Orsini and massively influenced by Charles II of Anjou, he was unanimously elected pope and crowned five days later. He did not follow the political line of his predecessor Boniface VIII, but his lack of firmness toward the Colonna family, along with pressure from France, forced him to flee to Perugia (April 1304) and made him revoke most of the measures taken by his predecessors (to the point of issuing a general absolution) or at least soften them (lifting the excommunication of Philip IV of France and his family, promulgation of the bull *Clericis laicos*). He wished to call to account (in the bull *Flagitiosum scelus*) only those directly responsible for the attack on Boniface VIII at Anagni—Guillaume de Nogaret and the Colonnas—but he died before promulgating the aggravated judgment of contumacy against the excommunicated men. He canceled the bull *Super cathedram* of Boniface VIII, which limited the pastoral activity of the mendicant orders. He enlarged the college of cardinals with three Dominican cardinals, since the order was practically his only source of support.

Clement V	1305–1314
John XXII	1316–1334
Nicholas V*	1328–1330
Benedict XII	1334–1342

Benedict XII (Dec. 20, 1334–Apr. 25, 1342, Avignon). Formerly *Jacques Fournier*, born ca. 1285 in Saverdun near Toulouse, studied in Paris (Master of Theology), in 1311 abbot of Fontfroide, in 1317 bishop of Pamiers, in 1326 bishop of Mirepoix; he led inquisitional proceedings against the Cathars. In 1327 he became a cardinal and theological advisor to John XXII—as the veteran theological expert and an eradicator of all forms of heresy, he was to end the dispute about the beatific vision, which had broken out in John's pontificate, with the dogmatic bull *Benedictus Deus* in 1336. After his election, the pope, who was inclined to moral strictness, began a comprehensive reform program, at whose center—along with a curial reform combating corruption, nepotism, and administrative abuses (attempts at reorganizing curial authorities; creation of better organizational and operational instruments for the system of penances and petitions; controversial limits on benefices, improving the selection of candidates through examinations)—was to be the reform of religious orders. From the outset resistance from the Dominicans blocked any thoroughgoing measures, so that apart from the general regulations against vagabond monks and crossing over from one order to another (1335), only slightly effective constitutions on discipline and organization for the Cistercians (*Fulgens sicut stella*, 1335), Benedictines (*Summi magistri*, 1336), Franciscans (*Redemptor noster*, 1337), and canons regular (*Ad decorem*, 1339) could be issued. Benedict's efforts to reorganize the papal states were highly promising, while his interventions in political matters were mostly unsuccessful (proceedings against Louis IV the Bavarian; attitude of the German electoral princes, Rhens 1338).

Clement VI	1342–1352
Innocent VI	1352–1362
Urban V	1362–1370
Gregory XI	1370–1378

Western Schism (Rome, Avignon, Pisa)

Urban VI [R]	1378–1389
Boniface IX [R]	1389–1404
Innocent VIII [R]	1404–1406
Gregory XII [R]	1406–1415
Clement VII [A]	1378–1394
Benedict XIII [A]	1394–1417

Benedict XIII (Sept. 28, 1394–July 26, 1417). Formerly *Pedro de Luna*, born in 1342/43 in Illueca from Aragonese nobility, professor of canon law in Montpellier, he was created a cardinal in 1375. At the outbreak of the Western Schism he was the member of the college of cardinals to whom Clement VII largely owed his recognition in France and the Spanish kingdoms. As pope he insisted uncompromisingly on his legitimacy, which, as a highly cultured person with wide literary interests, he justified in several works. As a way of resolving the schism he preferred the conquest of Rome with the violent removal of the opposition pope. In order to force Benedict to abdicate, the French besieged the papal palace in Avignon from 1398 to 1403. Negotiations over his resignation failed in 1408, and Benedict had to flee from Italy to the protection of the king of Aragón. The Councils of Pisa and Constance deposed him on June 5, 1409, and July 26, 1417, respectively, as a schismatic and a heretic. His life ended unnoticed in Peñiscola, probably on November 29, 1422. Two competing candidates were chosen to succeed him, Gil Sánchez Muñoz (Clement VIII) and Bernard Garnier (Benedict XIV).

Clement VIII*	1423–1429
Alexander V [P]	1409–1410
John XXIII [P]	1410–1415
Martin V	1417–1431
Eugene IV	1431–1447
Felix V*	1439–1449
Nicholas V	1447–1455
Calixtus III	1455–1458
Pius II	1458–1464
Paul II	1464–1471
Sixtus IV	1471–1484
Innocent VIII	1484–1492
Alexander VI	1492–1503
Pius III	1503
Julius II	1503–1513
Leo X	1513–1521
Hadrian VI	1522–1523
Clement VII	1523–1534
Paul III	1534–1549
Julius III	1550–1555
Marcellus II	1555
Paul IV	1555–1559
Pius IV	1559–1565
Pius V	1566–1572
Gregory XIII	1572–1585
Sixtus V	1585–1590
Urban VII	1590
Gregory XIV	1590–1591
Innocent IX	1591

Clement VIII	1592–1605
Leo XI	1605
Paul V	1605–1621
Gregory XV	1621–1623
Urban VIII	1623–1644
Innocent X	1644–1655
Alexander VII	1655–1667
Clement IX	1667–1669
Clement X	1670–1676
Innocent XI	1676–1689
Alexander VIII	1689–1691
Innocent XII	1691–1700
Clement XI	1700–1721
Innocent XIII	1721–1724
Benedict XIII	1724–1730

Benedict XIII (May 29, 1724–Feb. 21, 1730). Formerly *Pietro Francesco Orsini*, he was born on February 2, 1649, in Gravina di Puglia. He entered the Dominican order in 1667, receiving the religious name *Vincenzo Maria*. He was created a cardinal in 1672, in 1675 he became archbishop of Manfredonia, 1680 bishop of Cesena, 1686 archbishop of Benevento. Politically inexperienced, he was already weakened by old age when he became pope. In 1725 Benedict confirmed the bull *Unigenitus* and issued the bull *Pretiosus* in 1727. Mostly occupied with pastoral activity and canonizations, he largely abandoned other matters to the unscrupulous Cardinal Nicola Coscia.

Clement XII	1730–1740
Benedict XIV	1740–1758

Benedict XIV (July 7, 1740–May 3, 1758). Formerly *Prospero Lambertini*, born March 31, 1675, in Bologna. He combined talent, legal training, and an amiable nature with a flair for political reality and the requirements of the time. He entered curial service in 1701; by 1727 he was archbishop of Ancona, created cardinal in 1728, and made archbishop of Bologna in 1731. A competent, beloved pastor, as well as an author of important works, primarily about canon law, he was the surprise choice after a six-month conclave. As pope he was intent on reforms appropriate for the times and on reaching settlements with the European powers (agreement with Naples in 1741, Spain in 1753, Austria for Milan in 1757; recognition of the Prussian royal dignity). His decision in the bull *Ex quo singulari* (1742) requiring all Chinese missionaries to take a solemn oath against the rites proved to be a mistake. Along with administrative reforms in the papal states and the promotion of the arts and sciences, he busied himself in the domain of canon law, reforms in the liturgy, penitential practice, marital law, orders, curial authorities, as well as the Index of Forbidden Books. The encyclical *Annus qui* (1749) saw to the further development of church music. His works on beatifications and canonizations (*De servorum Dei beatificatione et beatorum canonisatione*, 4 vols. [Bologna, 1734–38]) and on the diocesan synod (*De synodo dioecesana* [Rome, 1755]) became fundamental texts in legal theory and practice. Benedict was the most important pope of his century and one of the most learned of all the popes.

Clement XIII	1758–1769
Clement XIV	1769–1774
Pius VI	1775–1779
Pius VII	1800–1823
Leo XII	1823–1829

Pius VIII	1829–1830
Gregory XVI	1831–1846
Pius IX	1846–1878
Leo XIII	1878–1903
Pius X	1903–1914
Benedict XV	1914–1922

Benedict XV (Sept. 3, 1914–Jan. 22, 1922). Formerly *Giacomo della Chiesa*, born November 21, 1854, in Genoa of old Genoese nobility. He became a close collaborator of the nuncio to Madrid and Cardinal Secretary of State Mariano Rampolla. Because of this collaboration he was more or less put on the shelf by Pius X. In 1907 he became archbishop of Bologna, but not until 1914 was he created a cardinal. After the serious diplomatic mistakes and internal church disturbances under Pius X (integralism, modernism, reform Catholicism), Benedict's pontificate introduced a period of necessary consolidation of the church in the older and newly established nation states; but it was entirely overshadowed by World War I and its consequences. In the war Benedict's efforts aimed at political neutrality, a just peace, and alleviating affliction (relief organizations for prisoners, exiles, and the destitute). In 1914 England and the Netherlands set up diplomatic missions with the Holy See, although Italy (on account of the unresolved Roman question) and France (since the separation of church and state in 1905) maintained no official contacts with the Vatican. The independence of the Vatican was respected by Italy, and Benedict opened a sort of branch office in Lugano for communicating with the Central Powers. The pope's early efforts for peace can be understood only in the framework of the complicated, often parallel and intersecting attempts at mediation by both governments and individuals. These efforts peaked, outwardly, in the peace note of August 1, 1917, but remained fruitless. Benedict was excluded from the peace negotiations, as the Allies had promised Italy in April 1915 that he would be. Benedict viewed the Treaty of Versailles as a vengeful dictate. He demanded justice even for the defeated and strove for reconciliation and internal peace within Europe, which included the necessary consolidation of the church in the older and newly established nation states. With the support of Cardinal Secretary of State Pietro Gasparri, the resolution of the Roman question and the reorganization of church–state relations were prepared by concordats. Along with the lessening of tension after the modernism crisis, the most important events within the church were the edition of the *Codex Iuris Canonici* (prepared by Pius X, promulgated in 1917, and in force from 1918) and the encyclopedia on the missions *Maximum illud* of November 30, 1919, with its future-oriented program for Catholic world missions.

Pius XI	1922–1939
Pius XII	1939–1958
John XXIII	1958–1963
Paul VI	1963–1978
John Paul I	1978
John Paul II	1978–2005
Benedict XVI	2005–

Material on the former "Benedict" popes is taken from the *Dictionary of Popes and the Papacy* © 2001, The Crossroad Publishing Company. Authors are Georg Schwaiger (I-IV, XIII-XV); Harald Zimmermann (V-VII); Klaus Jürgen Herrmann (VIII-IX); Tilmann Schmidt (X); Ludwig Vones (XI-XII); Dieter Girgensohn (XIII schismatic). The article "Benedict of Nursia," written by Pius Engelbert, is from the *Dictionary of Saints and Sainthood* © 2005, The Crossroad Publishing Company.

A Word from the Publisher

EDITORS AND BOOK PEOPLE concerned with theological writing have greeted Benedict XVI with excitement, or at any rate with great curiosity. The new pope is an intellectual of impressive clarity who was invited into the prestigious, and expressly secular, Académie Française. He is a believer of great depth and is said to experience the Catholic faith as nothing less than liberating. The name *Ratzinger* has often provoked strong reactions, whether praise or disagreement; but the precision of his thought seems to strengthen for others the ability to formulate and develop their own ideas. It is often said that theology is in one sense always partly biography. We hope this biography will enhance the reader's ability to fully appreciate the theological contributions of Benedict XVI.

Each of us will have his own encounter with Pope Benedict XVI. I am thankful for having had the opportunity to visit Cardinal Ratzinger a number of years ago, just a week before I was to move to New York City to become the publisher of The Crossroad Publishing Company. I was just a young novice sitting across from that velvet-red and gold bench in the cardinal's office, the same one seen in numerous photos published since the election. I asked the cardinal what he considered the most important issue facing the church with respect to the work of a Catholic publisher. I felt a bit awkward asking such a loaded question. But the cardinal appeared not to find it silly at all. He turned toward me in a focused and kindly personal way. Of the issues he named, I recall these words most clearly: "How do we respond to the question 'Who is Jesus Christ?'" He added that this was especially pressing in light of the encounter between Catholicism and representatives of Asian religious and philosophical thought.

Many of the cardinal's future challenges as Pope Benedict XVI were clearly outlined in this profound and comprehensive response. As in the choosing of the name *Benedict*—a name connoting, among other ideas, the powerful educational movement initiated by St. Benedict and a major force for social change in world history—this question he asked to answer my own was also to be understood symbolically. The inquiry about the person of Jesus Christ was not only a prerequisite for honest dialogue. After 2,000 years of speaking about Christ in a language formed by a Eurocentric and indeed Christocentric culture, it is at the beginning of this new century that our response to this matter will shape the future of our faith, and of the church.

The vision that underlies the pope's response to me has contributed to our 200-year tradition of publishing books that speak to the understanding of faith and the promotion of peace. We seek authors who can honor the particularity of their own tradition and articulate the challenges that are raised by dialogue. Our program aims to gather diverse reflections of that which is universal, "all that is Catholic," as one of our founders said, and communicate that diversity in a felicitous and edifying way.

It is in this passion of working with the word that I, the friends of the Press, and a writer who knows Joseph Ratzinger well proudly present this biography of Pope Benedict XVI.

GWENDOLIN HERDER

The Crossroad Publishing Company
invites you to discover more about
the life and thought of
Pope Benedict XVI.

In *The Yes of Jesus Christ: Spiritual Exercises in Faith, Hope, and Love*, Benedict XVI offers us a vision of Christian spirituality and the urgency of the Christian message. The "optimism" that lacks a Christian foundation cannot ultimately sustain faith, hope, and love. By exercising our spirituality through continual practice in Christian life, we hear again the distinctly Christian message that our ability to say Yes to ourselves and to one another can only come from God's Yes in Christ.

In *A New Song for the Lord: Faith in Christ and Liturgy Today*, Benedict XVI shows that liturgy is not a question just for specialists and historians—liturgy goes to the heart of our relationship to Christ, the Church, and ourselves.

In *Values in a Time of Upheaval*, Benedict XVI offers a wide vision of the basis of Christian morality, the right relation between Christian church and state, and other pressing political and social issues.